THE ROAD TO ORGANIC GROWTH

THE ROAD TO

ORGANIC GROWTH

How Great Companies Consistently Grow Marketshare From Within

EDWARD D. HESS

McGraw-Hill
New York   Chicago   San Francisco
Lisbon   London   Madrid   Mexico City
Milan   New Delhi   San Juan   Seoul
Singapore   Sydney   Toronto

7 8 9 10 11 IBT/IBT 1 9 8 7 6 5 4 3 2 1

ISBN 13: 978-0-07-147525-9
ISBN 10: 0-07-147525-7

This publication is designed to provide accurate and authoritative information in regard to the subject matter covered. It is sold with the understanding that the publisher is not engaged in rendering legal, accounting, or other professional service. If legal advice or other expert assistance is required, the services of a competent professional person should be sought.
> —*From a declaration of principles jointly adopted by a committee of the American Bar Association and a committee of publishers.*

McGraw-Hill books are available at special quantity discounts to use as premiums and sales promotions, or for use in corporate training programs. For more information, please write to the Director of Special Sales, McGraw-Hill Professional, Two Penn Plaza, New York, NY 10121-2298. Or contact your local bookstore.

This book is dedicated with gratitude to my mentors, who taught me the joy of both intellectual inquiry and intellectual honesty: Professor Sydney Jourard, Professor Charlie Davison, Professor Antonin Scalia, Jack McGovern, Peter Norton, Ira Wender, Professor Victor Zonana, Stuart Carwile, Bob Higgins, David Bonderman, Tom Aiello, Professor Bill Fulmer, Professor Lyle Bourne, and Professor Richard D'Aveni.

And this book is dedicated with love to Katherine, Jen, Sarah, Caroline, Ellie, Frankie, and Jackie.

CONTENTS

PREFACE

RGANIC GROWTH IS GENERATED BY MORE CUSTOMERS, new products, and operational efficiencies. Organic growth represents the underlying strength and viability of a business, whereas earnings generated by other means generally represent one-time transactions that have nothing to do with the company's core competencies, brand, or customer base—its earnings engine.

Intrigued by the financial scandals of recent history, I was motivated to research how many companies succeed by generating earnings the old-fashioned way—organically. That research, which I describe in detail in Chapter 1, took more than two years and required the use of a computer model to test the top 800 value-creating public companies on six criteria.

I expected that hundreds of companies would pass these tests. I was wrong. Less than 4 percent, or 22 companies, passed at least two of the three models. Those 22 winners piqued my interest—why and how did those companies do what 96 percent of the other big value creators could not do—grow primarily and consistently through organic means?

To answer this question, I began a second research project, described in Chapter 2, to discover why and how the 22 winners performed so well.

But I began that research with some biases. I expected that these 22 companies had better talent, visionary leaders, better strategies, unique products or services and were more innovative. I was wrong on all counts. In fact, those 22 companies do not necessarily have any of the aforementioned advantages. What they do have is the six keys to organic growth linked together into a consistent self-reinforcing system, which is the subject of the rest of this book.

In finding the six keys to organic growth, I also found that these companies managed the paradoxes of entrepreneurship and centralized control well, and they evolved through a common 12-step sequence or organic growth progression.

In this book you will find in-depth case studies about seven of those successful companies—American Eagle Outfitters, Best Buy, Outback Steakhouse, Stryker Corporation, SYSCO, Tiffany & Company, and TSYS. In addition, I discuss other winners—Walgreen, Wal-Mart, ADP, PACCAR, Gentex, Waters Corporation, Harley-Davidson, and Bed Bath & Beyond.

What I found was inspiring. It demonstrated that good (not necessarily the best) employees who are engaged and who are led by humble, passionate leaders can compete and win in the marketplace without unique products or services. Applying what I learned from these market leaders, I developed a roadmap of how to build a great, sustainable company to assist businesses both small and large.

I also came away questioning the role of management consulting firms, strategy consultants, and Wall Street in building great companies. Big change initiatives, big innovations, and diversification are not necessary to produce consistently high organic growth, according to my research.

Most of the 22 companies profiled here represent the best of American capitalism: humble, focused, and passionate competitors who have learned how to engage the human spirit (their employees) in the quest for operational excellence by treating people fairly.

What I hope you'll take away from this book is that you *can* build a sustainable and successful big business without playing accounting games or engaging in financial manipulations. And you can do it without commoditizing and devaluing your employees. The 22 companies studied here, in their own individual ways, reaffirm the American entrepreneurial spirit in that U.S. employees, if engaged properly, can outcompete any and all competitions.

ACKNOWLEDGMENTS

MANY PEOPLE AIDED IN THIS JOURNEY. Professors Robert Drazin, Robert Kazanjian, Greg Waymire, Al Hartgraves, Steve Stuk, and the following students deserve my gratitude for making my work better: Pete Bagwell, Christian Binder, Terence Brenan, Bryan Chitwood, Muhydine El-Jamil, Lyle Fogarty, Lauren Kelley, Michael Seeberg, Philip Weeber, Samuel Wineburg, Jason Hyman, Colin Jennings, Tamanna Dhankar, and Anuj Jaichand.

Thanks to Ron Harris, director of academic research computing at the Goizueta Business School, for programming, running, and providing quality control of the organic growth index model and to my research assistants, Ned Morgens, now an entrepreneur in Atlanta, and Catherine Keller, now a consultant at Deloitte & Touche.

To the executives and employees of the many companies who welcomed me and answered my endless questions, a big thank you. And a special thank you to Rick Schnieders, chairman and CEO of SYSCO, and to Mike Eskew, chairman and CEO of UPS, for their kindness in allowing me to study and write about their companies as my initial foray into the organic growth arena.

Thank you also to Lauren Foster of *The Financial Times* and to Ann Harrington of *Fortune* magazine for believing in and publicizing my work.

No book reaches its audience without the support and help of great editors. Jeffrey A. Krames, Jeanne Glasser, and Roger Stewart of McGraw-Hill are consummate professionals who challenged me and made my work better and who were true partners. And a special thanks to my editorial consultant Marcia Layton Turner, and Carol Gee. Thank you.

And thank you to Nanci Crawford, who for years has been the best executive assistant anyone could ever hope for and who now has worked with me on three books.

Most important, a special thanks to my wife, Katherine, who for over 25 years has encouraged me to take on professional opportunities that are challenging, interesting, and meaningful and who has endured lovingly too many moves, absences, and disruptions of her career for my work.

WHY IS ORGANIC GROWTH IMPORTANT?

ROWTH ACHIEVED THROUGH A COMMIT-
MENT to customer satisfaction, employee
engagement, and core profitability—*organic growth*—is a smart long-term strategy for any company. Organic growth represents the underlying strength and vitality of the core business and is created through economic value added; strong, increasing sales; and cash flow from operations above industry averages.

This is not to say that growth through mergers and acquisitions—*nonorganic growth*—is negative but that growth generated internally frequently results in better returns on investment, stock value improvements, lower employee turnover, and numerous other benefits you'll hear more about in the coming chapters.

How do I know this? I studied hundreds of companies to learn what differentiated those with consistent, organic high growth from those with sudden but often short-lived growth spurts. Long term, the companies that succeeded to a greater degree than their peers were found to follow an organic growth strategy.

NOT ALL EARNINGS ARE EQUAL

Surprisingly, few analysts and researchers have studied the merits or quality or character of organic growth versus growth through acquisitions. Some academic researchers looked at increasing revenues or increasing numbers of employees as evidence of growth. However, almost all academic research has counted every cent of earnings as equal, no matter how it originated, assuming the quality to be the same.

The first major attempt to evaluate the quality of business operating results was the Stern Stewart economic value-added computation, also known as the *EVA computation*, which is a proprietary formula that measures the value created by an asset or investment. A key component of the EVA calculation is a firm's net operating income after taxes. While analysts may argue that all earnings are equal, the EVA computation has been criticized because it relies on data that can be managed. However, its use has spread to the corporate world.

In an effort to restore confidence in corporate earnings statements following the all-too-familiar financial scandals of the early 2000s, in 2002, two Wall Street firms attempted to evaluate the quality and character of earnings. On May 14, 2002, Standard & Poor's (S&P) released its *core earnings test*, a methodology that separates a company's earnings into core and noncore classifications. While core earnings represented a significant step forward in evaluating earnings quality, it was criticized widely in the financial community and by some academics.

Merrill Lynch entered the fray with its *quality of earnings report,* created with Professor David Harkin of the Harvard Business School, that used four financial discriminating screens to evaluate the quality of earnings.

In 2003, my colleagues and I built the *organic growth index* (OGI), designed to identify companies with earnings generated organically rather than through earnings management or manipulation or through investment or financial engineering transactions (noncore) or acquisition.

BUILDING OUR MODEL

To start building the model, we studied in detail EVA, S&P's core earnings test, and Merrill Lynch's quality of earnings report. Then we talked to financial analysts at each of the respective firms. Next, we researched the academic literature on growth, earnings management, and earnings manipulation. We also talked with senior audit partners at major accounting firms to learn the common issues they faced in determining GAAP earnings. We then spent one year creating, assessing, and revising different tests to create the organic growth index (OGI), which is our extension of the work by Stern Stewart, S&P, and Merrill Lynch. We adjusted or incorporated into our model what we thought were the best parts of their work, and we added four new tests.

The reason for creating the OGI was multifaceted: We wanted to expand the definition of growth to include both sales growth and growth in cash flow from operations (CFFO). Second, we wanted a way to normalize results across industries, negating high margins resulting solely from industry choice. Third, we wanted to include an accounting manipulations test to highlight potential income adjustments, and last, we wanted to add a merger and acquisitions test to discriminate between serial acquirers who repeatedly purchased significant revenues from companies that grew internally or organically.

THE OGI STUDIES

Each of the three OGI studies consisted of six tests designed to identify value creators who outcompeted their industry competition primarily through organic growth. We started with the top 1,000 EVA companies for the base years 1996, 1997, and 1998, according to Stern Stewarts' EVA database and methodology. Our intent was to study the companies' growth performance during three five-year intervals: 1996–2001, 1997–2002, and 1998–2003.

We eliminated banks, diversified financial firms, real estate investment trusts (REITs), and insurance companies because of accounting and industry idiosyncrasies. After excluding those businesses, we were left with 834 companies in the 1996–2001 interval, 862 companies in the 1997–2002 interval, and 860 companies in the 1998–2003 interval.

TEST ONE

We then applied our first of six tests to companies in the study, computing an annual EVA per capital invested for each company and narrowing the list to the top 300 performers for each of the three time periods. We did this to adjust for size bias.

TEST TWO

In our second test, we examined both top-line and bottom-line growth, or sales growth and cash flow from operations growth. We determined the compound annual growth rate (CAGR) of sales for each company and compared it with the industry average. Then we looked at CFFO growth, determining which companies were increasing their cash flow from operations at rates greater than their industry's average; comparing performance against the companies' respective industries ensured that companies in high-margin industries were given no advantage over those in low-margin industries. This test assumed that reported CFFO is both an accurate measure of a company's growth and is less likely to be manipulated than financially reported net income.

We then calculated an industry-normalized statistic for both sales and CFFO growth and averaged the two. Companies with positive average z-statistics moved to the next test. After the second test, we were left with 170 companies from 1996–2001, 189 companies from 1997–2002, and 204 companies from 1998–2003.

By using EVA/capital invested and sales CAGR and cash flow from operations CAGR, we applied commonly accepted definitions of growth and economic value creation to identify growth companies. Now, having culled the top growth companies overall, we proceeded to test to eliminate nonorganic growers.

TEST THREE

Our third test applied Standard & Poor's (S&P) core earnings test to the companies remaining following the second test. S&P's core earnings measure is an attempt to identify income associated with a company's ongoing operations and excludes revenues or costs that arise from investments or nonoperating activities. It is an attempt to eliminate earnings manipulations common in corporate financial reporting. For our purposes, we equated a company's S&P core earnings with organic or internal growth, acknowledging that mergers and acquisitions activity was included by S&P.

We next performed sensitivity analysis using 90 percent as a possible "passing" grade—the S&P core earnings test indicates what percent of a company's growth is generated organically, and we set 90 percent as the minimum passing level. If a company's reported average net income deviated from the S&P average core earnings by more than 10 percent for the time period, we eliminated the company from continued consideration.

After the third test, we were left with 121 companies for 1996–2001, 106 companies for 1997–2002, and 128 companies for 1998–2003.

TEST FOUR

We then focused on aggressive accrual of income as a measure of growth. We looked at which companies were growing accounts receivables significantly faster than sales because a common accounting manipulation is to change income-recognition policies to accelerate sales revenue. Businesses can do this by granting more liberal credit to buyers, booking revenue earlier than previously booked in the transaction process, or forcing distributors or buyers to take products earlier than normal in the inventory turn cycle.

One method to determine whether these financial games are being attempted is to compare the growth rate of accounts receivables with the growth rate of sales. If accounts receivables are growing at a rate much faster than sales, it is a warning of aggressive accounting to boost sales revenues.

We compared year-by-year growth in both accounts receivables and sales for all the companies being studied, and if accounts receivables grew, on average, 10 percent or more than sales, we then looked at the relative size of accounts receivables versus sales. For the materiality standard, we chose 5 percent—that is, the total amount of accounts receivable must be greater than 5 percent of sales for the test to apply.

By the end of the fourth test, we were down to 93 companies in the 1996–2001 period, 69 companies in the 1997–2002 period, and 89 companies in the 1998–2003 period.

TEST FIVE

To the remaining companies, we applied Merrill Lynch's cash realization test, thereby eliminating companies reporting financial net incomes that exceeded cash flow from operations by 10 percent or more. The purpose of test five was to compare reported cash flow from operations with net income, assuming that the closer the two numbers are, the less likely a company has participated in earnings manipulations. We felt confident that this test, combined with the S&P core earnings test, would eliminate companies producing material financial results from sources other than organic growth.

Still, we needed a minimum acceptable percentage to identify the companies that were producing the highest organic growth. We settled on a hurdle rate of 90 percent and ended up with 87 companies in the 1996–2001 period, 62 companies in the 1997–2002 period, and 77 companies in the 1998–2003 period.

TEST SIX

To the remaining organizations, we applied a final test that eliminated companies that had acquired at least 33 percent of their increase in market value during the years in question. Because reliable mergers and acquisition data regarding the amount of income acquired generally were not available, we looked at deal values and compared the sum of the values of acquisitions made by a company during the applicable time period with the increase in its market capitalization for the same period. For this purpose, *market capitalization* was defined as total equity and debt capitalization.

When we were done with the final test, we were left with 39 companies for 1996–2001, 23 companies for 1997–2002, and 36 companies for 1998–2003 of the 834, 862, and 860 companies, respectively, that we had started with.

OGI WINNERS

The following are the specific companies that passed all six tests we applied for each of the three 5-year intervals:

1996–2001	**1997–2002**	**1998–2003**
1. American Eagle Outfitters, Inc.	1. American Eagle Outfitters, Inc.	1. American Eagle Outfitters, Inc.
2. Apollo Group, Inc.	2. Anheuser-Busch Cos., Inc.	2. American Pharma Partners, Inc.
3. Aptargroup, Inc.	3. Automatic Data Processing	3. Applebees International, Inc.
4. Arvinmeritor, Inc.	4. Bed Bath & Beyond, Inc.	4. Avon Products
5. Automatic Data Processing	5. Best Buy Co., Inc.	5. Bed Bath & Beyond, Inc.
6. Bed Bath & Beyond, Inc.	6. Brinker Intl., Inc.	6. Best Buy Co., Inc.
7. Best Buy Co., Inc.	7. C H Robinson Worldwide, Inc.	7. Biomet, Inc.
8. BJ's Wholesale Club, Inc.	8. Family Dollar Stores	8. Brinker Intl., Inc.
9. CEC Entertainment, Inc.	9. Gentex Corp.	9. Cognizant Tech Solutions
10. Chevron Texaco Corp.	10. Harley-Davidson, Inc.	10. Columbia Sportswear Co.
11. Colgate-Palmolive Co.	11. Lincare Holdings, Inc.	11. Costco Wholesale Corp.
12. Devry, Inc.	12. Mylan Laboratories	12. Coventry Health Care, Inc.
13. Dollar General Corp.	13. NVR, Inc.	13. Del Monte Foods Co.
14. Dollar Tree Stores, Inc.	14. Omnicom Group	14. Dollar General Corp.

(continued)

1996–2001	1997–2002	1998–2003
15. EOG Resources, Inc.	15. Outback Steakhouse, Inc.	15. EOG Resources, Inc.
16. Ethan Allen Interiors, Inc.	16. Paccar, Inc. Stores	16. Family Dollar
17. Family Dollar Stores	17. Ross Stores, Inc.	17. Gentex Corp
18. Gentex Corp.	18. Ruby Tuesday, Inc.	18. Harley-Davidson, Inc.
19. Home Depot, Inc.	19. SYSCO Corp	19. Intl. Game Technology
20. Jack In The Box, Inc.	20. Tiffany & Co.	20. Lowe's Companies, Inc.
21. La-Z-Boy, Inc.	21. Walgreen Co.	21. NVR, Inc.
22. Leggett & Platt, Inc.	22. Wal-Mart Stores	22. Omnicom Group
23. Masco Corp.	23. Waters Corp	23. Outback Steakhouse, Inc.
24. Molex, Inc. Co.		24. Pogo Producing
25. Mylan Laboratories		25. Ross Stores, Inc.
26. Nike, Inc.		26. Ruby Tuesday, Inc.
27. Omnicom Group		27. Ryland Group, Inc.
28. Outback Steakhouse, Inc.		28. Smucker (JM) Co.
29. Paccar, Inc.		29. Stryker Corp.
30. Renal Care Group, Inc.		30. SYSCO Corp.
31. Stryker Corp.		31. Tiffany & Co.
32. SYSCO Corp.		32. Total System Services, Inc.
33. Teleflex, Inc.		33. Urban Outfitters, Inc.
34. Timberland Co.		34. Walgreen Co.
35. Total System Services, Inc.		35. Wal-Mart Stores

1996–2001	1997–2002	1998–2003
36. Walgreen Co.		36. XTO Energy, Inc.
37. Wal-Mart Stores		
38. Waters Corp.		
39. WellPoint Health Networks, Inc.		

These tests produced 23 companies that were winners in two or more of the three time periods, and those companies are listed here in alphabetical order followed by their stock symbol. Ten companies were winners in all three intervals and are so noted with an asterisk following the stock symbol.

Company Name	Stock Symbol
1. American Eagle Outfitters, Inc.	AEOS*
2. Automatic Data Processing, Inc.	ADP
3. Bed Bath & Beyond, Inc.	BBBY*
4. Best Buy Co., Inc.	BBY*
5. Brinker International, Inc.	EAT
6. Dollar General Corporation	DG
7. EOG Resources, Inc.	EOG
8. Family Dollar Stores, Inc.	FDO*
9. Gentex Corporation	GNTX*
10. Harley-Davidson, Inc.	HDJ
11. Mylan Laboratories, Inc.	MYL
12. NVR, Inc.	NVR
13. Omnicom Group, Inc.	OMC*
14. Outback Steakhouse, Inc.	OSI*
15. PACCAR, Inc.	PCAR
16. Ross Stores, Inc.	ROST

(continued)

Company Name	Stock Symbol
17. Stryker Corporation	SYK
18. SYSCO Corporation	SYY*
19. Tiffany & Company	TIF
20. Total Systems Services, Inc. (TSYS)	TSS
21. Walgreen Co.	WAG*
22. Wal-Mart Stores, Inc.	WMT*
23. Waters Corporation	WAT

Note: I subsequently eliminated Dollar General from inclusion because it agreed in 2005 in a Securities and Exchange Commission (SEC) civil investigation that it had misreported income during the time period 1998–2000.

GROWTH QUESTIONS

1. How would your company do applying these six OGI tests?
2. What percent of your earnings do you produce organically?
3. Have you asked your investor relations person questions about the magnitude of your organic earnings?
4. Do you understand all the myriad ways your company creates earnings?
5. Is your company a serial acquirer?
6. Does your company change its income reporting or sales credit policies frequently?

2

DISCOVERING THE DNA OF ORGANIC GROWTH

TO BE INCLUDED ON THE ORGANIC GROWTH IN-DEX (OGI) LIST is certainly impressive—in fact, less than 4 percent of the companies studied in my three models during the years 1996–2003 passed all six organic growth performance tests. However, if you are an inquisitive person, you are probably asking how these 22 winners performed compared with the market.

HOW WELL DID THE 22 COMPANIES PERFORM?

The 22 companies on the organic growth index (OGI) performed well in comparison with major stock market indices.

OGI WINNERS COMPARED TO INDICES (1996–2003)

	NASDAQ 100	DJIA	S&P 500	OGI Companies
Cumulative returns	159.74%	100.91%	80.30%	779.05%
Annualized returns	12.7%	9.1%	7.6%	31.2%

SOURCE: OGI returns were calculated based on information from the University of Chicago CRSP database at the Center for Research in Security Prices.

In addition, the Securities and Exchange Commission (SEC) requires that companies compare their stock performance for the past five years with a major index and with a peer group. The numbers are normalized to start at 100. Here are the ending comparable results using the indices comparison—for which most companies use the S&P 500.

Both the indices and the company values started at 100 and in 2004 or 2005 ended as shown below.

Company	Ending Value for Company's Peer Group (rounded)	Ending Company Stock (rounded)
American Eagle	42	210
ADP	89	83
Bed Bath & Beyond	95 (est)	310 (est)
Best Buy	95	164
Brinker	89	202
EOG	100	422
Family Dollar	90	142
Gentex	59	139

(*continued*)

Company	**Ending** Value for Company's Peer Group (rounded)	**Ending** Company Stock (rounded)
Harley-Davidson	88	193
Mylan Laboratories	100	190
NVR	103	1611
Omnicom	89	89
Outback Steakhouse	91	182
PACCAR	89	485
Ross Stores	93	446
Stryker	89	280
SYSCO	89	185
Tiffany	85	87
TSYS	89	152
Walgreen	87	144
Wal-Mart	91	99
Waters	110 (est)	170 (est)

OGI winners also generated an average return on equity that surpassed—and in some cases far surpassed—their peers for the period 1999–2004.

AVERAGE RETURN ON EQUITY (ROE): RANKING

Company	Average ROE 1999–2004
NVR	90.84%
Waters	41.21%
SYSCO	33.54%
Ross Stores	32.58%
American Eagle	30.88%

Company	Average ROE 1999–2004
Harley-Davidson	30.71%
Omnicom	29.09%
Bed Bath Beyond	28.34%
Best Buy	26.43%
Stryker	25.29%
TSYS	24.21%
Wal-Mart	23.43%
Family Dollar	22.83%
EOG	22.27%
Tiffany	21.50%
PACCAR	21.07%
Walgreen	20.41%
ADP	20.23%
Gentex	19.77%
Outback Steakhouse	17.89%
Brinker	16.27%
Mylan Laboratories	15.91%

SOURCE: Thomson One Banker.

THEIR SECRET

How were these 22 companies able to grow consistently and primarily through organic growth? Were they in the right industry at the right time? Was it a function of size? Was it strategy? Was it unique intellectual capital? Was it efficiencies of scale? Was it innovation?

Ask a sophisticated investor why any company is a good growth company, and you're likely to hear that the company has a "sustainable competitive advantage." Or it has a "unique market position," "unique products," "better management," a "size (scale) advantage," a "cheaper supply of raw materials," "cheaper labor costs," or "a better strategy" or it is "more innovative."

We decided to find out whether these factors were found consistently in these 22 companies. We began our research in the public records—SEC filings, annual reports, proxy statements, company press releases, business articles, company Web sites, industry publications, and analyst reports—studying the 22 companies and some comparables. The research looked at strategy, culture, history, structure, business model, supply chain, logistics and distribution, technology platforms, customers, customer management, inventory management, human resources (HR) policies, employee retention, employee satisfaction, employee stock ownership, quality controls, financial controls, leadership philosophy, acquisition strategies, innovation, research and development (R&D), the sequence of growth, the role of cost efficiencies, and the overall interrelationship of the preceding.

This information gathering and analysis took five of us more than six months. Each of the five people took a subsegment of companies and independently developed his or her own hypothesis. Then, as a team, we looked for common themes across companies and for inconsistencies to generate test hypotheses. Based on this information, we finalized six hypotheses and tested them against the individual companies using primary research methods such as phone interviews and on-site visits.

Seven of the companies on the list allowed me to spend time interviewing various employees and members of senior management. They include SYSCO, Stryker Corporation, Outback Steakhouse, Best Buy, TSYS, Tiffany & Company, and American Eagle Outfitters. Wal-

green, Wal-Mart, Waters, and PACCAR are also refer-
enced throughout the book.

Despite the fact that all 22 companies on the OGI list
passed the six organic growth tests, no two companies
were completely alike. While all are high-growth businesses, their strengths and weaknesses vary. And they are
all works in progress. Throughout this book we will discuss in detail those attributes that supported internal
growth at these organizations.

EXPECTATIONS

We've heard from strategy and management consulting
firms, Wall Street, and the business press that high-
growth companies generally have advantages over their
lower-growth counterparts, including:

1. Unique products or services
2. Being more innovative
3. Better talent and better leadership
4. A favorable supply of raw materials
5. Being the most efficient, low-cost provider
6. Having high-margin intellectual capital
7. Being strategically hypercompetitive
8. Being globally diversified
9. Having the lowest labor costs through off-shoring
   or outsourcing
10. Outsourcing all nonessential parts of their value
    chain
11. Being the most aggressive in redefining industry
    rules or standards

However, our research found no proof that these factors were required for a company to be a consistent high-performance organic grower. And in most cases, commonly held beliefs about organic growth simply were wrong.

The myths and truisms we discovered include

1. Contrary to popular belief, it is *not* necessarily a war for talent—you do *not* have to have the best people. But you do need high employee engagement—intensely focused, emotionally engaged employees who are committed to excellence. Employee engagement is mission-critical.

2. You do *not* necessarily need unique products or services. You do need good-enough products, great customer service, and great execution. All of these 22 winners are execution champions.

3. You do *not* necessarily need to control a unique supply of raw materials nor control a unique distribution channel.

4. You do *not* necessarily need sophisticated or diversified strategies; you do need a strategy or business model that the average line employees can understand. Most of the winners have a focused, narrow strategy.

5. You do *not* necessarily need to be an innovation leader with big breakthrough discoveries. You do *not* need a unique business model or major innovations, but you do need to constantly iterate and incrementally improve.

6. You do *not* necessarily need to have the lowest la-
    bor costs. Most of the OGI winners do not.
7. You do *not* necessarily need to be global. Many of
    the 22 winners have no international sales or op-
    erations.
8. You do *not* necessarily need to outsource or head
    off-shore.
9. You do *not* necessarily need an MBA to run your
    business. Only three of the 22 CEOs have MBAs.
10. You do *not* necessarily need a charismatic CEO.
11. You do *not* necessarily need to be located near tal-
    ent, raw materials, or customers.

Surprisingly, we found these oft-cited sources of competitive advantage to have little or no impact on building
a company fueled by consistent organic growth. In fact,
six other characteristics proved to be the true keys to
achieving sustainable organic growth.

THE SIX KEYS TO ORGANIC GROWTH

Our investigation found that these companies generally
possessed the six keys discussed below. We also learned
that these companies worked hard on creating a consistent, seamless, self-reinforcing internal system that drove
certain value-creating organic growth behaviors. Organic
growth is more than a strategy—it is an internal system.

AN ELEVATOR-PITCH BUSINESS MODEL
All 22 companies have a simple, easy-to-understand
strategy and business model that can be explained to and
understood by line employees. They also stay focused,

are disciplined, and "stick to their knitting" rather than pursue complex diversification strategies. And they evolve through incremental improvement. Big innovations, new business models, and changing industry dynamics or rules are not prevalent. They keep it simple and focus on growing the business incrementally.

INSTILL A "SMALL-COMPANY SOUL" INTO A "BIG-COMPANY BODY"

The second key is to be entrepreneurial at the point of customer contact. OGI winners give employees the power to act to meet customer needs, while having strong central controls over quality, supplies, finance, etc. What we found that was critical was giving people with customer contact the authority, power, responsibility, and accountability for results. The 22 companies push "ownership" of the customer down into the organization. And they successfully manage the paradoxes and tensions between entrepreneurship and central control. These companies structure themselves to promote entrepreneurial "ownership."

MEASURE EVERYTHING

The 22 OGI winners are measurement maniacs. They measure not only financial metrics but also key operational metrics (most daily) and behaviors. Metrics are necessary, but they become more value-creating when they are aligned with accountability and rewards. Metrics objectify employee performance and reduce corporate politics and favoritism. Like all companies, these companies do make mistakes. But because of their information and measurement systems, they know about them quickly and can make corrections quickly. They are resilient. They use met-

rics to give employees frequent feedback and therefore
can reduce variances or exceptions.

BUILD A PEOPLE PIPELINE

The companies have engaged, loyal employees and build
a multilayered talent pool. They obtain consistently superior performance from line employees on a daily basis
and have above-average employee loyalty and retention
rates compared with industry averages. And they get this
engagement without sacrificing accountability, standards, or quality. In most of these companies, employees
are treated fairly and with dignity and respect. High-
growth companies generally create an environment of
stability—regarding strategy and leadership—and em-
phasize iterative, be-better activities rather than large-
scale metamorphoses. This macro stability allows the
companies to promote from within, giving their employees defined career paths. Employees in these companies
"own" their results and their careers, and most even own
part of the company. These companies' management
teams are frequently home grown, with long company
tenures. Elitism is also rejected in these companies—the
trappings of imperial or regal CEOs are absent. For example, Best Buy, Walgreen, and Tiffany & Company have
no corporate jets or executive dining rooms.

LEADERS: HUMBLE, PASSIONATE, FOCUSED OPERATORS

These organic growth companies typically are led by
humble, passionate, internally focused operators. The
majority of these CEOs are not self-absorbed. They know
their success is due to the work of others. Few CEOs came

from elitist or privileged backgrounds—most were educated at state schools. Most are operators—engineering types. These leaders fight arrogance and complacency in themselves and their organizations. They are focused on the business—on the operations and on their many be-better initiatives.

BE AN EXECUTION AND TECHNOLOGY CHAMPION

OGI winners do not have better strategies than the competition. Most do not even have unique products or services. What they do better every day is *execute*. These companies have engineering-processed most of their value chain and, through technology, have become very cost efficient, productive, and knowledgeable about what is going on inside their companies.

They are into the minutia—high standards (99 percent error-free is the norm). These companies know that they are only as good as their last delivery and that they earn their customers one transaction at a time.

These companies use technology to drive efficiencies across their value chain. To them, technology is not a service function; it is an operational function. As such, technology professionals are integrated into functional areas in many of these companies.

THE SEAMLESS LINKAGE OF THE SIX KEYS

Skeptics may say, "Well, gee. Every company that is successful does some of these things." Yes, this may be true. But these 22 companies do *all* of these six things well and have evolved to a point where they have *seamlessly and consistently linked* these six keys together in a self-reinforcing manner. They are focused on a fundamental operating principle: *Engage the people closest to the customer in their daily pursuit of excellence.* We found that they grow organically because

1. They are execution champions.
2. They have better employee involvement, performance, and loyalty and lower turnover.
3. They have institutionalized a consistent, be-better, entrepreneurial environment throughout their culture and into functional areas, measurement processes, accountability, and reward systems.
4. They have learned how to be cost efficient and highly productive without destroying employee engagement.
5. They are world-class technology companies.
6. Their leaders are focused on the operations of the business.

High organic growth companies work as hard or even harder on getting the internal processes right as they do on market-facing activities. Consequently, their growth rate is generally higher and more consistent than the majority of their competition.

Food marketing giant SYSCO follows the six keys every day. SYSCO is the total package—a growth-execution champion led by humble, focused operators.

THE SYSCO STORY: "AN ENTREPRENEURIAL MARKET LEADER"

Based in Houston, Texas, SYSCO is the largest food marketing and distribution company in North America. The company sells more than $30 billion of food, and related products and services annually to more than 400,000 customers through 157 separate profit centers, employing a total of 46,000 employees.

The magnitude of its operations is immense. SYSCO sells more than 300,000 products and delivers almost 4 million cases of food and related food service products to 360,000 customers every day, 99 percent on-time and defect-free. More than half the company's 46,000 employees are hourly warehouse and delivery people, and approximately 12,000 are in sales and business development.

Despite the fact that the food distribution industry has low margins, SYSCO's financial statistics are impressive. Its annual sales growth has outpaced food service industry growth by two to three times on a consistent basis.

The company's 20-year compounded annual growth rate through 2004 was 14.6 percent. Fiscal year 2004 sales increased 12 percent, whereas net earnings were up 17 percent. The company has consistently paid a dividend since its inception and has increased the quarterly cash dividend 36 times in 35 years. Return on equity, which was 22.2 percent in fiscal year 1998, reached 38.7 percent in fiscal year 2004, whereas return on average capital has grown steadily from 15.0 to 24.9 percent during the same time period. During the last six fiscal years, SYSCO returned approximately $3.6 billion to shareholders via dividends and share repurchases.

From fiscal year 1984 through 2002, the company's compound annual sales growth rate was over 9 percent, compared with an industry average of 2.6 percent. Its available market space is approximately $207 billion. With sales of almost $30 billion, it has an approximately 15 percent market share.

SYSCO is the major player in a $200 billion market—although it has only a 15 percent market share. Not only is it big, but it outperforms its industry competition year in and year out.

What makes the company different is that its leaders have figured out, on a daily basis, how to get and keep everyone—from the CEO to the truck driver—focused on doing the little things that count very, very much to their customers.

Simply put, SYSCO is an execution champion. It has figured out how to balance and manage the tensions between decentralized entrepreneurial autonomy and centralized controls. The company has figured out how to measure what is important to its success and how to reward it all the way down the chain to paying productivity incentives to truck drivers on a weekly basis.

It is a "quiet" company without a lot of cheerleading or corporate frills. More like successful farmers than Wall Street stars, management gets up every day, goes to the fields, tills the soil, waters, fertilizes, pulls the weeds, harvests some crops, and gets up the next day and does the job again and again very well. Managers go about the business of doing business in a determined, engaged, and methodical way.

CONSULTATIVE SELLING

SYSCO has the largest sales force in its industry, all focused on the customers and customer segments in which it can add the most value, deepen relationships, and increase profitability. Its sales people visit their key accounts, on average, three times a week. And stories abound regarding occasions when the company's sales people pitched in to help customers by washing dishes, waiting tables, etc. when employees unexpectedly did not come to work. They support their customers in many ways, including bringing their own families to their customers' eating establishments. They build business relationships and friendships that yield more revenue growth and higher profits through stability.

The company recently introduced a new business review process featuring in-depth reviews with the company's most valued customers. Its purpose is to determine the customer's wants and needs, see what is working and what is not working, and provide recommendations to help the customer's business become more profitable. The business-development teams also focuses on acquiring new customers by targeting high-potential accounts currently doing business with the competition.

The company also established a relationship management initiative called "Customers Are Really Everything to SYSCO" (CARES), a program designed to make certain that its customers receive the best service in the basic functions that customers need to run their business, such as receiving all products ordered, on time, and in undamaged condition; receiving accurate invoices; having helpful and knowledgeable sales and delivery associates; and receiving the quality assurance inherent in SYSCO-brand products.

The CARES program has evolved into its second phase, *i*CARE, in which marketing associates are trained to be more effective business consultants for their customers. They are trained to understand a food service operation's profitability model, thereby enabling them to analyze and develop menus, control inventories, and provide food safety training for SYSCO customers. Through the company's Web site, customers are also able to access a variety of third-party services to help them drive and increase customer traffic, such as access to potential lenders to fund expansions or restaurant upgrades; assistance in creating guest birthday cards, table tents, banners, or posters; and even access to insurance carriers, credit-card services, and other services that normally might be cost-prohibitive.

A PAY-FOR-PERFORMANCE CULTURE

SYSCO employees, from the CEO to the warehouse worker, understand the mission: "Helping Our Customers Succeed." But why is SYSCO so much more profitable than its competitors? Is it just efficiencies of scale? Or is it something else? The company's major advantage boils down to its seamless integration of its entrepreneurial culture and its performance measurement and reward system.

SYSCO SERVICE PROFIT CHAIN

	Work Climate Average	Operating Pretax Percent	Operating Expense as a Percent of Sales	Workers' Comp Percent of Sales	MA Retention	Delivery Retention	Associates per 100,000 Cases
Top 25% work climate at SYSCO units	4.01	7.5%	13.3	0.07	85	88	4.13
Bottom 25% work climate at SYSCO units	3.61	5.3%	14.9	0.20	72	78	4.33
Variance	0.40	2.2%	1.6%	0.13	13	10	0.20

The service profit chain rings true at SYSCO. Companies with highly satisfied associates deliver better.

SYSCO employees know that their job is to "Help [Their] Customers Succeed" and what the performance expectation is. They know that the company measures what is important and that employees will be financially rewarded for meeting or exceeding performance objectives.

Through years of iteration and just plain hard work, SYSCO has demonstrated that "people will do what you measure," and they will do it even better if rewarded.

SYSCO'S ENTREPRENEURIAL CULTURE

SYSCO's entrepreneurial culture is emphasized on a daily basis through

- *Ownership.* Sixty-five percent of its employees own stock (a share of the results of their hard work) in the company.

- *Autonomy.* Its 157 operating units have day-to-day authority to operate in their market, subject to strict central financial controls and measurement.

- *Employee retention.* Information sharing and collaboration across business units leads to the industry's best retention rates. SYSCO reports a retention rate of 82 percent for sales people and drivers, the key customer-facing positions. At the officer level, retention rates exceed 99 percent, with an average tenure of more than 20 years.

- *Promoting from within.* The company fills more than 95 percent of its open positions by promoting from within the company. In addition, six of its top seven executives are former line operators within its own business units.

HUMAN CAPITAL AT SYSCO (2004)

Level	Retention Rate	Average Tenure, years	Average Age, years
Executive Vice President & above	100%	22	55
Senior Vice President	100%	26	54
President	97%	23	51
OPCO Executive Vice President	98%	20	48
Specialty MIP	93%	21	49
Corporate Vice President	100%	20	52
Corporate AVP	93%	12	48

Rich Schnieders, chairman and CEO of SYSCO, states that "this culture is self-replicating. Our people feel good because many own stock, and they see results when everyone works hard and performs. Many, including our truck drivers, are on incentive bonus programs and see compensation results directly and weekly. All this makes people work harder—they feel good about the results which they share in, and then they feel good about working hard tomorrow."

The company's focus on its operations—the blocking and tackling of its business—is evidenced also in how its CEO spends his time.

Mr. Schnieders spends his time as follows:

- 30 percent—customer relationships, including direct responsibility for three major accounts

- 20 percent—internal corporate processes, for example, measurement and supply chain

- 20 percent—specific company operating issues

- 10 percent—supplier relationships

- 10 percent—external, that is, Wall Street and investor relations

- 10 percent—industry leadership matters

SYSCO's customers are clearly at the core of the company's operational processes, down to driving how the CEO spends his time. He knows that the time spent with customers will yield the greatest rewards in terms of performance for himself and for the company as a whole.

MEASUREMENT AND REWARD SYSTEMS
While SYSCO allows its 157 business units to operate "the front of the house" autonomously, the back of the house is centralized—controlled with a sophisticated measurement system.

SYSCO's emphasis on metrics is evidenced by the fact that its top 10 executive officers meet every Wednesday afternoon and review several hundred metrics for every one of the 157 operating units' prior week's performance. The company measures "everything" related to the receipt, movement, and delivery of products and services to its customers, new business development, every expense and capital expenditure, and its return on equity.

These metrics are made possible by a central system implemented in 1995, the SYSCO Uniform System (SUS), which it developed internally. The building of the SUS gave the company the ability to mine data on its customers and to use those data to provide better service while using its resources more efficiently. SUS also made it possible to stratify its customer base and determine which customers were the most profitable.

A performance-based system must have strong financial controls, and SYSCO maintains a tight rein, requiring that operating company financial results and a myriad of operational and performance metrics be reported to executive management each week. While the companies are operated autonomously, they benchmark extensively on performance and operational metrics and share best practices in all areas of the business with peer operating units within the corporation because it is difficult to find external comparables. The operating units compete with each other for operational recognition and rewards. Likewise, operational units strive not to be on the weekly Wednesday watch list of "underplan" performers.

The SYSCO measurement system drives the performance-based culture. SUS is used to determine rewards and reinforce local autonomy and the entrepreneurial spirit. The culture and the measurement system go hand in hand. Every one of its 170 top managers, including its top 10 executives, is paid a salary at the 25th industry percentile, but they have the opportunity to earn a bonus that can put their total compensation at the 75th industry percentile. The company's 2,500 top operating company managers work on an incentive reward system too. And the company is now implementing this incentive reward system at the truck driver and warehouse employee level.

CHAIN OF GROWTH

SYSCO's DNA—the internal design that makes the company unique—is the seamless integration of its culture and measurement and rewards systems. These systems drive and focus behavior.

How has SYSCO been able to produce year-in and year-out stellar growth? Its growth chain evolved slowly. First, the company grew by expanding its geographic footprint until it covered every major U.S. market. Most of this growth occurred prior to 1988, through the acquisition of many small, local family-owned food distribution businesses. Once SYSCO had its geographic footprint, it then divided the customer market into four segments and created cost-efficient products for each customer segment, from the high-end luxury restaurant to the fast-food carryout restaurant. Then it entered the ethnic food business—Chinese, Italian, Mexican, Asian—and the specialty foods business—high-end beef and organic fresh vegetables. After rounding out its product offerings within the four customer segments, the company expanded into distributing the hard goods its customers needed. Customers found it easier, more efficient, and more reliable to place one order with SYSCO than multiple orders with multiple vendors. Its evolution continued from food to products to the services needed by its customers, including menu design and operational consulting.

The company then focused on its margins—how it could use technology to operate more efficiently. It measured and iterated until it focused on 15 to 20 key value-driving metrics responsible for the bulk of its value creation. Today, this journey continues: SYSCO is completely redesigning its supply distribution logistics system into major regional centers to simplify supplier logistics and maximize delivery efficiencies at significant cost savings.

ROLE OF ACQUISITIONS

SYSCO's last large acquisition was in 1988, when it acquired CFS and became a national distributor. The company has been acquiring companies since it was formed, although much of its growth is not attributable to its acquisitions. While acquisitions have been important to establish critical geographic footholds, it has grown faster internally than by acquisitions.

The fact that the company has the resources and the internal structure to support the acquired companies in achieving continued growth has been a strength. When making an acquisition, SYSCO usually seeks the premiere distributor in a particular market, typically structuring its acquisitions with an earn-out provision over a period of years, which motivates the seller to stay involved, maintaining profitability during the assimilation.

It has been a critical metric for the company's shareholders that acquisitions be nondilutive of earnings. SYSCO typically expects any acquisition to be nondilutive of earnings within the first couple of years. Acquisitions are chosen based not only on their position in the market but also on what they may bring to the table, such as a location that fills a particular geographic gap or a particular product base.

In 35 years, SYSCO has made approximately 121 acquisitions. In 1999, the company began looking at specific distributors to fill customer product needs. Since then, not only have broadline distributors been acquired but also niche distributors, such as nine meat operations, four fresh produce operations, an Asian cuisine specialty company, a distributor to the lodging industry, and a sub-

sidiary that specializes in supplying internationally located chain restaurants. Some may be operations that
function as a stand-alone facility, whereas others may be
"folded into" an existing SYSCO profit center.

FUTURE GROWTH OPPORTUNITIES
SYSCO's long-term financial objectives include growing
sales in the low- to middle-teens percentage range, with
acquisitions contributing an average of 3 percent annually. The company wants to leverage earnings growth so
that it outpaces sales growth while maintaining a 35 percent return on equity and maintaining a 35 to 40 percent
debt-to-total-capital ratio.

How can the company do this? First, the company
only has a 14 to 15 percent market share of a $200 billion
market. And, on average, it has only captured 33 percent
of its existing customer total food service buys. As CFO
John Stubbefield stated, "Eighty-six percent of the customers out there do not think we are the best. And those
who do still buy more products combined from others
than they do from us."

So SYSCO's prime growth opportunities, according to
former President Tom Lankford, are

1. "Acquiring new key customers.
2. Selling more products to existing customers and
    driving the 33 percent penetration to 60 percent.
3. Adding more specialized disposable products and
    ethnic foods.
4. Restructuring the supply chain to reduce costs
    substantially so [that] we can compete in the $20
    to $40 billion market of very small customers
    without lowering our profit margin.

5.   Expanding internationally, where we have less than 1 percent of our business—especially to the U.K. and Europe."

The company's leadership has not become complacent or arrogant, even with great success. They, like their warehouse employees, drivers, and sales force, do business the SYSCO way—by trying to be better today in helping their customers succeed. It is this improvement mentality that is reinforced through an integrated measurement and compensation system that makes SYSCO a formidable competitor.

GROWTH QUESTIONS

1. How many of the six keys to organic growth does your company meet?
2. What are your company's variances with this model?
3. Are responsibility, authority, power, accountability, measurement, and rewards linked in your organization?
4. What parts of your value chain have you not engineer-processed using world-class technology?
5. Are your leaders humble and detail- and execution-focused operators?
6. Do you feel that you have a career path at your company?
7. Who "owns" the customer in your company?
8. Can you explain your business in a simple sentence?
9. How engaged are your employees?
10. What trappings of power or elitism does your CEO enjoy?

3

THE ORGANIC GROWTH WINNERS: INTERESTING FACTS

FOR YEARS, STRATEGY CONSULTANTS HAVE ADVO-CATED that sustainable competitive advantages can be created by locating businesses near nodes of complementary supporting businesses, supplies, or labor pools. Likewise, economists have advocated the necessity of size, which created economies of scale. And the business education system and business press have extolled the merits of having an MBA degree.

In this chapter I'll explain why these commonly held beliefs do not always hold true when applied to the 22 high organic growth performers.

DOES LOCATION MATTER?

You do not need to be located in a major city near suppliers, universities, or a highly educated labor pool. More than

50 percent of the *organic growth index* (OGI) companies are not based in a top 10 metropolitan area, and some are in fairly remote towns. The smallest cities represented are Columbus, Georgia (TSYS), Bentonville, Arkansas (Wal-Mart), and Kalamazoo, Michigan (Stryker), where companies still were able to build technology-based businesses despite being located large distances from major technology centers, universities, and a high-tech employee base.

And neither coast seemed to present a particular advantage because the headquarters of the 22 winners are rather evenly distributed across the United States. Of the 22 high organic growth companies studied, 7 were headquartered in the Midwest, and 5 were based in the Southeast region of the United States. New England and the New York City area accounted for 5 winners, whereas the Southwest had 3 companies, and the West Coast, surprisingly, was the laggard with 2 companies.

OGI COMPANIES RANKED BY METROPOLITAN POPULATION

Specifically, where are the 22 companies located? The following chart lists the metropolitan area of each of the corporate headquarters for the OGI model winners, according to the U.S. Census.

Company Name	Location	Metro Area (as Defined by U.S. Census)	Metro Area Population (2000 U.S. Census)
Bed, Bath, & Beyond (BBBY)	Union, NJ (Newark)	New York–northern New Jersey—Long Island, NY—NJ—CT—PA CMSA	21,199,865

Company Name	Location	Metro Area (as Defined by U.S. Census)	Metro Area Population (2000 U.S. Census)
Omnicom Inc. Group, (OMC)	New York, NY	New York–northern New Jersey—Long Island, NY—NJ—CT—PA CMSA	21,199,865
Automatic Data Processing (ADP)	Roseland, NJ (Newark)	New York–northern New Jersey—Long Island, NY—NJ—CT—PA CMSA	21,199,865
Tiffany & Co. (TIF)	New York, NY	New York–northern New Jersey—Long Island, NY—NJ—CT—PA CMSA	21,199,865
Walgreen (WAG)	Deerfield, IL (Chicago)	Chicago—Gary—Kenosha, IL—IN—WI CMSA	9,167,540
NVR, Inc. (NVR)	McLean, VA (Washington, DC)	Washington, DC—Baltimore, MD—VA—WV CMSA	7,608,070
Ross Stores (ROST)	Pleasanton, CA (Oakland)	San Francisco—Oakland—San Jose, CA CMSA	7,039,362
Waters Corporation (WAT)	Milford, MA (Boston)	Boston—Worcester—Lawrence, MA—NH—ME—CT CMSA	5,819,100
Brinker International (EAT)	Dallas, TX	Dallas—Forth Worth, TX CMSA	5,221,801
SYSCO (SYY)	Houston, TX	Houston—Galveston—Brazoria, TX CMSA	4,669,571
EOG Resources	Houston, TX	Houston—Galveston—Brazoria, TX CMSA	4,669,571

(continued)

Company Name	Location	Metro Area (as Defined by U.S. Census)	Metro Area Population (2000 U.S. Census)
PACCAR, Inc. (PCAR)	Bellevue, WA (Seattle)	Seattle—Tacoma—Bremerton, WA CMSA	3,554,760
Best Buy (BBY)	Richfield, MN (Minneapolis)	Minneapolis—St. Paul, MN—WI MSA	2,968,806
Outback Steakhouse (OSI)	Tampa, FL	Tampa—St. Petersburg—Clearwater, FL MSA	2,395,997
American Eagle (AEOS)	Warrendale, PA (Pittsburgh)	Pittsburgh, PA MSA	2,358,695
Mylan Laboratories (MYL)	Cannonsburg, PA (Pittsburgh)	Pittsburgh, PA MSA	2,358,695
Harley-Davidson (HDI)	Milwaukee, WI	Milwaukee—Racine, WI CMSA	1,689,572
Family Dollar Stores (FDO)	Matthews, NC (Charlottle)	Charlotte—Gastonia—Rock Hill, NC—SC MSA	1,499,293
Gentex Corporation (GNTX)	Zeeland, MI (Grand Rapids)	Grand Rapids—Muskegon—Holland, MI MSA	1,088,514
Stryker Corp (SYK)	Kalamazoo, MI	Kalamazoo—Battle Creek, MI MSA	452,851
Wal-Mart Stores (WMT)	Bentonville, AR (Fayetteville)	Fayetteville—Springdale—Rogers, AR MSA	311,121
Total System Services (TSS)	Columbus, GA	Columbus, GA—AL MSA	274,624

SOURCE: www.census.gov/population/cen2000/phc-t3/tab03.xls.

Notice the small number of California companies (1) and the small number based in Chicago (1), Philadelphia (0), Los Angeles (0), Atlanta (0), Miami (0), Dallas (1), Seattle (1), and Denver (0). Notice that 15 of the 22 companies are based in the "heartland," not on either coast. Wal-Mart, TSYS, and Stryker support the contention that you can build a great high-performance company anywhere.

I submit that location is not a key factor in building a consistent high-performance company. Most of these companies ended up in their areas by happenstance or personal circumstances, not by strategic choice or study. Now let's look at the size of the winners. How many are megacap companies? Size becomes important because many corporations espouse the view that once they achieve a certain size, it is difficult to maintain consistent high-performance organic growth, and thus they have to make big acquisitions.

DOES SIZE LIMIT ORGANIC GROWTH?

Size is a complicated issue for many companies. It is common knowledge that there is a minimum size needed to gain operating efficiencies and that, at some point, a company becomes more difficult to manage as it grows. Likewise, at some point, size makes adaptability and speed of market response an issue.

Interestingly, the OGI companies focused not on their size but on the size of their underlying market. And second, the companies kept trying to expand their overall market by moving along the organic growth progression to new market segments. Other key size findings we made were that Wal-Mart challenges the view that organic growth is limited predominantly to a company's infancy and adolescent stages. And most of the OGI companies moved up a market capitalization classification as my research was being conducted.

These 22 companies employ between 1,250 (EOG) and more than 1,700,000 (Wal-Mart) employees. Excluding Wal-Mart, though, which is a statistical outlier, the other 21 companies employ an average of 35,000 people, and 7 of the 22 employ in the neighborhood of 50,000 people.

LARGEST EMPLOYERS

Company	No. of Employees (rounded)	Return on Equity (1999–2004)
Wal-Mart	1,700,000	23.43%
Walgreen	160,000	20.41%
Best Buy	100,000	26.43%
Brinker	100,000	16.27%
Outback	70,000	17.89%
Omnicom	60,000	29.09%
SYSCO	50,000	33.54%

SMALLEST EMPLOYERS

Company	No. of Employees (rounded)	Return on Equity (1999–2004)
Harley-Davidson	8,500	30.71%
Tiffany	7,300	21.50%
TSYS	5,200	24.21%
Waters	4,200	41.21%
NVR	3,900	90.84%

Company	No. of Employees (rounded)	Return on Equity (1999–2004)
Mylan	2,450	15.91%
Gentex	2,100	19.77%
EOG	1,250	14.10%

What is interesting about the seven largest employers is that, except for Omnicom, they have all figured out how to get consistent high performance from primarily hourly workers. Many megacap companies use size as the reason why they must grow nonorganically.

Besides number of employees, market capitalization is another way to look at these companies. As the following chart shows, the average market capitalization of the 22 companies is approximately $22 billion, as of 2004, ranging from Wal-Mart at $224 billion to Gentex at nearly $3 billion. Eleven companies, or half the winners, had market capitalizations below $10 billion.

OGI COMPANIES RANKED BY 2004 MARKET VALUE

Rank	Company Name	2004 Market Value (millions)
1	Wal-Mart Stores (WMT)	$223,685.50
2	Walgreen (WAG)	$39,190.38
3	Automatic Data Processing (ADP)	$25,860.34
4	SYSCO (SYY)	$24,420.89
5	Best Buy (BBY)	$19,494.21
6	Stryker Corp (SYK)	$19,397.60
7	Harley-Davidson (HDI)	$17,848.22
8	EOG Resources (EOG)	$16,972.98
9	Omnicom Group. Inc. (OMC)	$15,711.08

(continued)

Rank	Company Name	2004 Market Value (millions)
10	PACCAR, Inc. (PCAR)	$13,981.23
11	Bed Bath & Beyond (BBBY)	$11,986.07
12	Waters Corporation (WAT)	$5,654.05
13	Family Dollar Stores (FDO)	$5,237.49
14	NVR, Inc. (NVR)	$4,894.15
15	Total System Services (TSS)	$4,783.43
16	Mylan Laboratories (MYL)	$4,757.73
17	Tiffany & Co (TIF)	$4,651.63
18	Ross Stores (ROST)	$4,237.81
19	American Eagle (AEOS)	$3,471.88
20	Outback Steakhouse (OSI)	$3,376.96
21	Brinker International (EAT)	$3,031.55
22	Gentex Corporation (GNTX)	$2,874.68
Average		**$21,614.54**

In our study, 18 of the 22 companies have a market capitalization of between $2 and $20 billion. Wal-Mart is a megacap company, 10 are large-cap companies, and 11 are midcap companies. During the time frame studied, many of the companies moved up the capitalization classification chart, except for Wal-Mart. This upward movement in capitalization classification should not be surprising because these companies grew organically at rates much higher than their industry competition during the period in which we were studying them. And the marketplace rewarded that growth with substantial stock appreciation. This capitalization movement does create an interesting research opportunity: Finding small-cap and midcap companies that exhibit the six keys may well present a good investment opportunity for someone. Of course, this assumes that the capitalization movers are able to sustain their high organic growth over long periods of time, as these 22 companies have done.

DO YOU HAVE TO BE GLOBAL?

No one disputes that the world has become a smaller place, primarily owing to the Internet linking countries, companies, and individuals almost everywhere. Globalization has commoditized capital, labor, products, and now knowledge workers or intellectual capital. Does a high-performance organic growth company have to operate globally?

No. The 22 OGI winners actually are split into two groups with respect to this issue—operating heavily internationally or operating almost exclusively domestically. The first group, with significant international sales, consists mainly of vertically integrated manufacturing companies with intellectual property in a narrow market. Companies in this camp include Waters Corporation— liquid chromatography and mass spectrometry equipment; Tiffany & Company—fine luxury jewelry; Stryker Corporation—orthopedic implants and equipment; PACCAR—medium- and heavy-duty trucks; and Gentex— electrochromatic rearview mirrors.

Company	Percent of Sales International (rounded)
Waters	67%
Omnicom	50%
Gentex	50%
Tiffany	40%
Stryker	35%
PACCAR	34%

The rest of the companies, the second group, have much smaller or minimal international sales.

Company	Percent Sales International (rounded)
Wal-Mart	19%
Harley-Davidson	18%
TSYS	18%
ADP	17%
Best Buy	10% (Canada)
American Eagle	7% (Canada)
Bed Bath & Beyond	0%
Brinker	N/A
Family Dollar	0%
Mylan Labs	0%
NVR	0%
Outback Steakhouse	N/A
Ross Stores	0%
SYSCO	0%
Walgreen	0%

Interestingly, two retailers, Wal-Mart and Tiffany, both have major operations in Japan, and both operations are performing below expectations. The companies doing well internationally generally are selling specialized products through a highly trained sales force. Maybe business models that rely on hourly workers at the point of customer contact do not transfer well to other cultures because employee engagement processes and policies can be culturally influenced. Clearly, though, based on this information, having a strong international operation is not a determinant of strong organic growth.

WHO LEADS THESE COMPANIES?

To achieve such impressive organic growth, you might assume that these companies must be led by well-educated MBAs. Wrong. Of the 22 companies on the OGI list, only three of the CEOs have MBA degrees—the CEOs of PACCAR, Tiffany, and EOG. Of the 22 CEOs, 14 have undergraduate degrees rather than a graduate degree and none from an Ivy League university.

Company	CEO's Undergraduate Degree from
Best Buy	University of Denver
NVR	Ashland University
Walgreen	North Dakota State University
Wal-Mart	Pittsburgh (Kansas) State University
Omnicom	Adelphi University
SYSCO	University of Iowa
Outback	University of Kentucky
Brinker	University of Houston
TSYS	Louisiana State University

Great companies can be led by non-MBAs and by students of almost any college. The lesson here is that a top-ranked school education or an MBA does not appear to be a necessity to lead a high-performance company.

CEO WORK EXPERIENCE

In this fast-paced global world, do you have a better chance of becoming a CEO at a high-performance organic growth company if you succeed at a previous employer? If you've worked in more than one industry? Apparently not.

Many of the CEOs of the 22 companies studied started at the bottom of the hierarchical ladder at their company and spent more than 20 years working their way up to the CEO position in that same company. Of the four "aberrations," three had deep industry expertise before joining their current company.

CEO of	Tenure with Company (in years)
NVR	36
Harley-Davidson	33
Best Buy	32
Gentex	31
PACCAR	28
Walgreen	28
Brinker	27
Wal-Mart	26
ADP	25
Waters	25
SYSCO	23
Tiffany	22
TSYS	22
EOG	21
Omnicom	21
Ross	16
Family Dollar Stores	15
Bed Bath & Beyond	13
American Eagle	6
Outback	6
Mylan	3
Stryker	2

The CEO tenure chart is powerful. It illustrates the value of growing your internal leadership team and, in most cases, also demonstrates the benefit of stable, consistent leadership in high organic growth companies. On average, the CEOs of these 22 companies had a tenure of 20 years at their respective companies. Most also grew up in the company and knew the business inside and out. The 4 companies that recently brought in outsiders to take over were American Eagle, Stryker, Outback Steakhouse, and Mylan.

HOW DO THESE COMPANIES FINANCE ORGANIC GROWTH?

Growth initiatives—organic or not—require capital. Many of these companies at some point went public to access public equity capital for growth. But now they produce growth capital primarily from cash flow. On average, they have less than a 5 percent debt-to-market-capitalization ratio, and only 4 companies have long-term debt that exceeds more than 10 percent of their market capitalization. Those companies are Wal-Mart, PACCAR, Omnicom, and Brinker.

ARE THE CEOS PAID TOP DOLLAR?

Excluding stock option exercises, the average total compensation for these 22 chief executives was $4.8 million. According to the most recent (as of December 2005) proxy statements filed with the Securities and Exchange Commission (SEC), they had the following total compensation—*excluding* any stock options they may have exercised:

Company	CEO Compensation
Wal-Mart	$17.5 million
Harley-Davidson	$11.4 million
Bed Bath & Beyond	$8.8 million
Waters	$7.1 million
American Eagle Outfitters	$7.0 million
ADP	$6.2 million
SYSCO	$5.5 million
Walgreen	$5.2 million
Omnicom	$5.2 million
PACCAR	$4.7 million
Family Dollar Stores	$3.5 million
NVR	$3.4 million
Stryker	$3.4 million
EOG	$3.0 million
Mylan	$2.8 million
Tiffany	$2.6 million
Best Buy	$2.5 million
Gentex	$1.7 million
TSYS	$1.4 million
Ross	$1.0 million
Outback	$.8 million
Brinker	$.7 million

Excluding stock options exercised, many of these CEOs were not the top-paid people in their industry, even though, in some cases, they were the top performer. This challenges commonly held assumptions about the need for boards of directors to continually raise CEO pay, even for average or poor performance. Interestingly, these high-performance CEOs do not leave their companies to go elsewhere for more pay. Nor do they generally use their companies as springboards to vault into the zone of mega-CEO pay.

ARE THESE CEOS' FINANCIAL INCENTIVES ALIGNED WITH THEIR SHAREHOLDERS?

In almost all cases, the CEOs owned as of the last proxy filed (as of December 2005) significant stakes in the companies they manage.

Company CEO	Company ROE 1999–2004 (%)	CEO Tenure with Company (years)	CEO Stock Owned (rounded)
Stryker	25.29	27	$976 million
NVR	90.84	36	$379 million (founder)
Family Dollar Stores	22.83	15	$324 million (father was founder)
Best Buy	26.43	32	$225 million
PACCAR	21.07	28	$180 million (founding family)
Waters	41.21	25	$157 million
Outback	17.89	17	$128 million (founder)
Wal-Mart	23.43	26	$106 million
EOG	22.27	21	$86 million
Bed Bath & Beyond	28.34	13	$72 million
ADP	20.23	25	$65 million
Harley-Davidson	30.71	33	$64 million
Gentex	19.77	31	$54 million (founder)

(*continued*)

Company CEO	Company ROE 99–2004 (%)	CEO Tenure with Company (years)	CEO Stock Owned (rounded)
Tiffany	21.50	22	$46 million
Mylan	15.91	3	$29 million
American Eagle	30.88	6	$27 million
TSYS	24.21	22	$26 million
Ross Stores	32.58	16	$22 million
Brinker	16.27	27	$21 million
SYSCO	33.54	23	$20 million
Walgreen	20.41	28	$18 million

Stock ownership appears to be a powerful tool for these companies. And many have employees as well as CEOs as actual stock owners, which is different from owning stock options. First, investors can track when a CEO disposes of stock. And second, many of these CEOs have a substantial part of their net worth tied to the company.

CONCLUSIONS

Studying these high organic growth companies produced insights that challenged commonly held views about strategy, the importance of location, the necessity to be a global company, and the importance of a diverse job history for a CEO. Likewise, the necessity to pay exorbitant compensation to hire or retain good CEOs was questioned.

The leaders of these companies, in general, are very humble people, many from nonprivileged backgrounds who have not forgotten where they came from. The business press and others have created the illusion that good business leaders have MBAs and are larger-than-life individuals who deserve the pay they receive. Yet we have seen that the leaders of the 22 organic growth companies do not fit that mold.

I submit that size, location, globalization, and compensation theories are as often used as excuses for poor performance rather than being requirements for high performance.

GROWTH QUESTIONS:

1. How does your CEO's pay compare with the pay of these CEOs?
2. Is off-shoring or outsourcing made a necessity for some companies by their poor management?
3. PACCAR, Stryker, Tiffany, and Waters have significant manufacturing operations in the United States (and not in the Sunbelt). What does this say?

AN ELEVATOR-PITCH BUSINESS MODEL

WHILE EVERYONE AGREES THAT AN EF-FECTIVE BUSINESS MODEL is critical for success and growth, the 22 companies on the *organic growth index* (OGI) list take it one step further—their business models are simple and easily understood. More important, their employees are able to communicate the company's business model clearly and concisely to virtually anyone. With simplicity comes understanding and engagement because employees know where the company is headed, how it will get there, and what their individual role is in that growth. Employees understand why their job is important and how it fits into the big picture. Simplicity is what makes consistent high growth possible.

These companies keep it simple and focused, and they keep the focus consistent or stable over long periods of time. With the big picture clear, everyone from the CEO on down knows how to perform on a daily basis from a big-picture or macro perspective while incrementally improving the micro details of execution daily.

Four characteristics these companies have in common are

1. They are generally in one business—most can define their business in one sentence.
2. The companies are relentlessly focused and disciplined—they do not take their eye off the ball.
3. They drill down to the line-employee level to ensure that their people understand the business and why their job is important, why certain measurements are being made, and how employees can contribute to their own success.
4. They incrementally improve with continual top-line and bottom-line initiatives.

All this is made feasible and attainable because the business strategy is focused—it is narrow. It is distilled into a concisely and clearly enunciated business model that line employees can understand. Understanding that at any given time there is a limit to how much people can focus on, these companies keep it simple.

The OGI companies are not bouncing from one major initiative or one management fad to another. Their macro system generally is stable. Yet these companies are not complacent. They improve incrementally. They constantly adapt the details of execution—but not the strategy, business model, leadership, internal rules of the game, or what is most important.

And it all starts with the simplicity of their business model.

WHAT IS THE ELEVATOR PITCH?

Can an employee explain the business in an elevator ride? If he or she can, the company has made its model and strategy clear to all. Let us look at the 22 companies on our list to see if they all meet these criteria:

1. ADP sells front- and backoffice outsourcing administrative solutions.
2. American Eagle sells value fashion merchandise to 15- to 25-year-olds.
3. Bed Bath & Beyond sells quality domestics and home furnishings.
4. Best Buy sells and services branded consumer electronics, appliances, home office equipment, and entertainment products.
5. Brinker is a casual dining restaurant company.
6. EOG finds and distributes natural gas.
7. Family Dollar Stores sells low-priced products to low- and middle-income consumers.
8. Gentex designs, manufactures, and sells automobile rearview mirrors.
9. Harley-Davidson manufactures and sells motorcycles, motorcycle parts, and related apparel and accessories.
10. Mylan Laboratories creates, manufactures, and sells generic pharmaceuticals.
11. NVR builds, sells, and finances homes.

12. Omnicom is a holding company selling corporate advertising, marketing, and communication services.
13. Outback is a casual dining restaurant company.
14. PACCAR designs, manufactures, sells, and finances medium- and heavy-duty trucks.
15. Ross Stores sells off-price branded merchandise to middle-income consumers.
16. Stryker designs, manufactures, and sells orthopedic implants and surgical equipment.
17. SYSCO sells food and restaurant-related products and services to food service establishments.
18. Tiffany designs, manufactures, and sells fine jewelry and luxury goods.
19. TSYS processes credit cards and sells customer relationship management services.
20. Walgreens is a convenience pharmacy chain.
21. Wal-Mart operates a low-cost, high-volume retail distribution system.
22. Waters Corporation designs, manufactures, and sells high-performance liquid chromatography and mass spectrometry instruments for the pharmaceutical and life-science industries.

Simple and focused. That is the key.

PRODUCT FOCUS

Some of our winners are focused by product type, such as Gentex, which generates 82 percent of its revenue from selling rearview mirrors to the automobile industry. Stryker focuses on orthopedic and reconstructive surgery implants, equipment, and related products. Waters Corporation makes specific laboratory research equipment. Harley-Davidson makes motorcycles. TSYS primarily processes credit cards. Tiffany primarily sells fine jewelry. PACCAR sells medium- and heavy-duty trucks. NVR builds, sells, and finances homes.

CUSTOMER-FOCUSED

Other companies may sell many different products or SKUs but are focused on a particular customer segment:

SYSCO	Food establishments
American Eagle	15- to 25-year-olds
Brinker	Midmarket casual diners
Outback Steakhouse	Midmarket casual diners

VALUE PROPOSITION FOCUS

Some companies sell many different products to many different customer segments but rely on a simple value proposition to define themselves:

ADP	Cost-effective front- and backoffice outsourcing
Best Buy	Sells solutions for electronic products for the home and office
Mylan Laboratories	Sells generic drugs
Walgreen	Sells convenience
Wal-Mart	Sells value at the lowest cost

EVOLUTION

Not all these companies were so focused when they began or as they evolved. For example, historically, American Eagle operated two very different retail concepts. NVR used to be in the land-assembly and lot-development business too. Walgreen was a miniconglomerate before Charles Walgreen III decided to focus on pharmacies and exited the discount store, travel agency, optical center, and fast-food restaurant businesses.

Gene Cassis of Waters Corporation summarizes the company's commitment to focus: "We are very disciplined—we are aware of the danger of being good at nothing" if we diversify. And Stryker Corporation's 27-year record of 24 percent compound annual growth is attributed to a "relentless focus on our core business."

THE ABSENCE OF THE BIG WOW

With few exceptions, such as Stryker's purchase of Howmedica in 1998, these companies do not engage in big changes—big deals—or big innovations. New business models, changing industry structures, or introducing revolutionary or unique products or services is not what distinguishes these companies.

What does distinguish them is that they execute every day very, very well. They are into the "blocking and tackling" of business. They are into the minutia—the details of every critical process in their value chain. They are not complacent. On the contrary, they try to get better and better, little by little. They are incremental. They evolve.

They create a be-better culture that overcomes compla-cency and boredom. And they focus as much or even more on internal processes, systems, and linkage as they do on external market-facing activities.

Lee Scott of Wal-Mart said it best in a 2003 *Financial Times* interview:

> Wal-Mart is a story of evolution, not revolution. When I came in 1979, we spent most Friday mornings at our meetings talking about what TGNY was doing, what Gibson Discount was doing, what Kmart was doing, what JC Penney was doing, what Sears was doing. The whole thing was based on taking the best elements of those stores—so much of what we have done has been things we actually saw other people doing and inte-grated into what we were doing. All of those things have just kind of incrementally, month-by-month, year-by-year, come together to create something that is interwoven and meaningful. Individual decisions at the time those decisions were made were not in strat-egy sessions that laid out, 12 years from now—here's what we'll look like and we'll put these individual pieces together along this schedule to achieve this goal. We are the masters of incrementalism.

If these companies grow incrementally, how do they do it? Is there a common sequence or progression? In fact, there is.

Nearly all the 22 OGI companies followed the com-mon progression of organic growth described next. They took similar steps to achieve solid, consistent organic growth.

THE COMMON PROGRESSION OF ORGANIC GROWTH

In studying these companies, an unanticipated finding was what I call the *organic growth progression* or *sequence:* the steps taken by these companies to continuously drive organic growth. And some of the companies even went through the steps in the same progression or order despite being in different businesses or industries. This progression or sequence is a good roadmap or checklist for any business wanting to achieve consistent organic growth.

Step		Action
1	↓	You expand your business geographically.
2	↓	You introduce complementary products for existing customers.
3	↓	You move into a new customer segment with your products.
4	↓	You add complementary services for existing customers.
5	↓	You focus on cost efficiencies.
6	↓	You focus on technological productivity in the supply-chain, logistics, and manufacturing functions.
7	↓	You use technology to focus on customer knowledge and service.
8	↓	You then focus on people measurement, hiring, and training.
9	↓	You add or acquire a complementary new concept.
10	↓	You change from a product company to a customer-solutions company.
11	↓	You start over at step 1.
12		You simultaneously improve in all 10 areas yearly.

THE PROGRESSION OF ORGANIC GROWTH

Although these companies generally followed this progression, there are four key points to understand. First, the progression along the organic growth chart chain is industry- and business-specific. Second, at some point, the company engages in more than one step at a time. Third, at some point, the company starts over and revisits all the previous steps to reassess each step for more growth. Last, at some point, most companies have improvement initiatives occurring simultaneously across several steps.

This sequential order of organic growth is part of the companies' strategy rather than a by-product. These companies have a simple, easy-to-understand business that they have grown primarily organically. One can say that their organic growth strategy is represented by this sequence of organic growth—even though on day one none of the companies envisioned the sequence.

Simply put, their strategy is to acquire more customers, then to sell more products and services to those customers, then to enter a new customer segment, and then to focus on cost efficiencies and productivity. Then they decide how to leverage their competencies so that their products or services are not commoditized. This is how the 22 OGI winners did it—and how you can, too. Let's look more closely at each stage of the progression.

GEOGRAPHIC EXPANSION

The fastest way to grow is by geographic expansion. Geographic expansion can occur by opening new sales locations or by entering new markets. Successful geographic expansion requires disciplined execution processes that allow one to execute replication consistently and efficiently, what I call *replicution*—executing replication.

Can you quickly open up a new location, on time and within budget, and operate it profitably? You can if you have disciplined execution processes. After the initial geographic expansion, these companies look at adopting smaller size formats to enter smaller markets or different markets from the ones that fueled their initial growth.

For example, American Eagle has a domestic expansion program and acquired a chain in Canada. Bed Bath & Beyond, Family Dollar Stores, Ross Stores, Best Buy, Tiffany, Wal-Mart, and Walgreen have domestic expansion programs. Is geographic expansion finite? Theoretically, yes. Some firms recalibrate market saturation and learn that they can have many more stores in an area than conceived previously, as was the case with Walgreen and Best Buy. Or some may introduce different size formats in different demographic areas, as Best Buy, Wal-Mart, Outback, and Brinker have tried. Some may look internationally, as Wal-Mart and Tiffany are.

The manufacturing companies—Gentex, Harley-Davidson, PACCAR, Stryker, and Waters—also have expanded internationally via sales forces, marketing offices, acquisitions of foreign product companies, acquisitions of distribution facilities, and acquisitions of manufacturing facilities.

ADDING NEW PRODUCTS FOR EXISTING CUSTOMERS
Adding new products your customer base needs or wants is the second step. American Eagle, for instance, added

lingerie for its 15- to 25-year-old customers. Bed Bath & Beyond added Christmas decorations. Family Dollar Stores added milk and other perishables. Wal-Mart added groceries, hardware, and low-end luxury items. Harley-Davidson added apparel and accessories. Omnicom added marketing services. ADP added front-office out-sourcing solutions. Stryker added surgical supplies, and TSYS added customer relationship management tools.

ADDING NEW CUSTOMER SEGMENTS

Pursuing new segments beyond the company's core base is the next stage. ADP expanded into the brokerage in-dustry, small businesses, and automobile dealers. NVR went downmarket with its homes. SYSCO expanded into ethnic and specialty foods. Wal-Mart went after the small-business market with its Sam's Club subsidiary, and Brinker and Outback both expanded concepts to pene-trate different ethnic niches, such as Italian food.

ADDING COMPLEMENTARY SERVICES

After geographic expansion and adding more products for existing customers, some companies seek to spur top-line growth by adding complementary services to their core product offerings. Best Buy added the Geek Squad to ser-vice its computer and digital products. Harley-Davidson, NVR, and PACCAR added financing units. Stryker added physical therapy services for its orthopedic patients. SYSCO added menu planning and restaurant management services. TSYS added customer relationship services. Wal-green added photography processing, and Wal-Mart is con-sidering going into the banking business.

FOCUSING ON COST EFFICIENCIES AND PRODUCTIVITY

After companies grow the top line, many face what I call the *growth wall*. Can they keep growing at the same pace? Can they increase market share at the same pace? At some point, increasing market share means taking market share from others.

To avoid having such growth become a zero-sum game, companies begin focusing on generating earnings by becoming more cost efficient and productive. Such efficiencies enable some companies to enter lower-priced market segments without sacrificing margin. Wal-Mart is the world champion at this game. Even for other companies, though, this move follows a similar pattern.

Cost-efficiency and productivity initiatives involve technology and engineering processes. High-growth companies effectively become technology companies by pursuing cost efficiencies and productivity throughout their value chain. Ultimately, they define themselves as technology companies. These high organic growth companies have implemented cost-efficiency and productivity initiatives in a sequential order, focusing first on their supply chain, then moving on to distribution logistics, and then to customer relationship management, ending with human resources initiatives focused on hiring and measuring accountability.

ADDING A NEW CONCEPT

Before starting over at the bottom of the chain, some companies attempt to redefine themselves from a product-driven company to a customer-solutions company. SYSCO and Best Buy are in different stages of this type of transformation, whereas TSYS is just beginning.

It is a major challenge. Employees have to be taught new skills—listening, analytical and diagnostic skills, patience, and a service mentality that deems that the right solution for the customer is better than the highest-margin product.

Best Buy has a major customer-centric solutions initiative under way currently. With new competition from Wal-Mart and others, Best Buy understands that the consumer of electrical components for the home and office has many choices, some of which are highly complex. To better meet its customers' needs, the company determined that it needed to provide its customers with more help and undertook a massive research project to segment its core customer base into five segments. Each customer segment was given a name, such as Buzz, Ray, Barry, and Jane. Employees are now trained to diagnose the needs of the customer and to provide a complete end-to-end solution for that customer based on the segment they are determined to fall within.

This approach required that Best Buy change its centralized structure back to decentralized, giving the store managers and point-of-customer-contact people the freedom, flexibility, and responsibility to meet customer needs. Customer needs are now paramount—not the product and not the margin—and Best Buy is receiving high marks for this new approach.

ENTREPRENEURIAL NEW CONCEPTS

Five of our 22 winners have or are engaged in starting up new concepts. Brinker and Outback, for example, are veterans of starting or buying restaurant concepts in their infancy, testing them, and then deciding whether to roll them out nationally.

Ross Stores is also testing a new complementary concept; American Eagle has announced that it is in the process of opening an entirely new concept—Martin & Os; and Tiffany & Company has created a new concept called *IRIDESSE*, a pearl jewelry store.

CONCLUSIONS

High-growth companies have a simple, understandable business model that their employees can understand and execute—none has a complex or sophisticated strategy. The business grows through incremental steps along the organic growth progression. But all these companies stick to their business.

Despite being simple, the business models these companies follow have created world-class competencies in technology enablement, engineering processes, and replication. Many of the companies, including Wal-Mart, Walgreen, Tiffany, SYSCO, PACCAR, Harley-Davidson, American Eagle, and Best Buy, are best-of-class in these competencies.

Almost all these companies have world-class competencies in logistics and distribution and manage thousands of employees in different locations efficiently and with real-time operational metrics. Their focus on execution processes, operations, and technological enablement of their value chain is a lesson in and of itself. The organic growth winners focus as much or more on these things as they do on strategy. Their strategy evolves incrementally.

THE STRYKER STORY: "A UNWAIVERING FOCUS ON 20 PERCENT GROWTH"

Stryker Corporation, based in Kalamazoo, Michigan, is one of the world's leading orthopedic medical device companies, with sales approximating $5 billion, 16,000 employees, and an amazing track record of 24 percent compound annual growth rate (CAGR) earnings per share over the last 28 years. Since 1977, Stryker grew from $17 million in sales to nearly $5 billion led by John Brown, a chemical engineer who built an organic growth "execution machine."

THE STRATEGY

The Stryker strategy and culture are based on four simple principles:

1. Results speak louder than words.
2. Do not lie, cheat, or steal.
3. Grow the earnings per share 20 percent a year.
4. Take responsibility and be accountable for what you do.

In 2004, Stryker recently codified these principles as

The Stryker Promise:	Deliver exceptional results
Pillars:	Constant improvement, culture of accountability, winner's intensity, and innovation that endears service ethic
Personality:	Driven
	Honorable

	Committed
	Direct
Performance:	Actions
	Behavior
	Command

HISTORY

Stryker was founded in 1941 by Dr. Homer Stryker with $20,000 and an idea for a product. Dr. Stryker was a caring doctor who became an inventor in order to help his patients. His motto was, "Never create a product for profit alone."

Dr. Stryker's first invention was the Stryker turning-frame bed, which is still used widely today; it allowed nurses and attendees to mechanically turn nonambulatory patients. He also invented the oscillating saw, which could cut through a patient's cast without cutting his or her limb.

In 1955, Dr. Stryker's son, Lee, became general manager of the company, and in 1958, the company sold $1 million of products through a direct sales force. Less than 20 years later, by 1976, Lee Stryker had built the business to $17 million in sales but was soon after tragically killed in a private plane crash.

The board of directors searched for a replacement and found John Brown, an engineer working for Squibb, as a CEO candidate to fill Lee's shoes. However, Brown turned down the board's offer, fearful of being left out in the cold if the family were to sell the company later.

But the board kept calling him, hoping that he would change his mind. Finally, one board member asked

Brown what it would take for him to accept. Brown answered, fully expecting and wanting the person to go away, that he needed more ownership—approximately 5 percent. The board said, "Done deal." That was December 1976.

TWENTY PERCENT A YEAR

When Brown joined Stryker in 1977, he had one primary short-term goal—to go public. By going public, you could be positioned as an emerging growth company, and Brown did so in 1979.

During the initial public offering (IPO) process, a senior investment banker asked Brown how much growth was necessary to be an emerging growth company, and Brown responded that he did not know. The investment banker answered his own question—20 percent. This answer became Brown's strategy, vision, mission, and objective.

The goal quickly became the assumption—the specific objective by which winning was defined. It was a stretch goal, but Brown believed that people performed best when pushed to be better, to do more. But he also wanted a counterbalance to the drive and persistence he was instilling in the company, which was his code of conduct. Simply put, it stated that Stryker employees do not lie, cheat, or steal. And for 25 years, 20 percent annual growth and John Brown's code of conduct were the Stryker culture, mission statement, core values, and strategy. Simple, easy to understand, and consistent.

STRYKER TODAY

Today, Stryker is a leader in the areas of hip, knee, shoulder, spinal, and microimplants; bone cement systems for implants, medical devices, and trauma products, including external fixation systems and hip fracture devices. Stryker's microimplant devices are specially developed to reconstruct facial and hand deformities, and its orthobiologics division has been researching regenerative products for more than 20 years. Finally, its instruments division is a world leader in surgical tools and equipment.

Although the company employs 16,000 people, its headquarters staff consists of just 75 people overseeing 14 divisions. Its products are manufactured in the United States and overseas, with approximately 35 percent of its revenues being international.

John Brown is the first to acknowledge that Stryker's significant growth and success were the result of being in a growth industry. Even so, the growth has been dramatic:

Year	Sales
1977	$13 million
1981	$43 million
1985	$100 million
1990	$280 million
1993	$550 million
1997	$980 million—21 consecutive years of 20% earnings growth
1998	Big acquisition
1999	$2.1 billion
2002	$3.0 billion
2004	$4.3 billion

Stryker's organic growth occurred as a result of increasing market share, adding new product lines, adding complementary products, and ultimately, adding personal therapy services. Although Stryker historically bought technologies to use as a platform for new products, in 1998 it bought Howmedica from Pfizer, thereby doubling its size and coming close to knocking it out of the model as an organic growth winner (versus acquisitions-generated growth).

Today, it owns 19 percent of the knee implant market, 24 percent of the hip implant market, 7 percent of the spinal implant market, 18 percent of the trauma market, 15 percent of the microimplant market, and 47 percent of the base cement market.

During the last 28 years, Stryker has had a compound annual sales and earnings per share growth rate of 24 percent; its current market capitalization exceeds $19 billion. Today, the Stryker family owns approximately 30 percent of the company, and John Brown and other executives own about 10 percent. The company has created more than 120 employee millionaires. About 27 percent of its employees own stock individually, and an additional 1.6 million shares are owned in retirement plans.

ENTREPRENEURIAL STRUCTURE

Although Stryker clearly has achieved significant organic growth, the first five years of John Brown's tenure were challenging. During that time, Brown was a micromanager, involved in and controlling everything. But eventually he became frustrated at how long things were taking to implement and realized that he was the real problem.

To eliminate himself as the bottleneck to progress, Brown decentralized the business and, as he says, put everybody "in the fishbowl." He gave his division heads complete authority to run their own show as long as they hit the 20 percent growth target. He made them "owners" of their businesses because they were closest to the customer.

Brown kept control through his reporting process, which included 7:00 a.m. Monday informational meetings, which ran anywhere from 30 minutes to several hours, during which each leader reported to senior management about sales, quality control, supply and service, customer complaints, and budget numbers.

In addition, every month every leader handed in a detailed formal report outlining activities, successes, and failures. Likewise, Brown spent three days a month preparing a 10- to 12-page formal written report to the board summarizing the same, which was distributed to all leaders.

Transparency, accountability, and the burden of responsibility on the people closest to the customer produced an owner mentality and an execution culture at Stryker. The strategy was simple. The issue was one of execution.

What Brown did was institutionalize a stretch goal of 20 percent growth per year and push responsibility and accountability down the organization through decentralization. Both actions created a "we need to be better" culture. This relentless cultural pressure to grow precluded Stryker from becoming complacent or arrogant.

Brown managed by focusing on the gaps, today called *variances*, or who was having trouble meeting the 20 percent number. Brown's hiring principle was as simple as his growth strategy and his code of conduct: He hired smart, hard-working people who got along well with others.

Brown managed his employees by putting them in positions to play to their strengths. The international business, for example, was built by a manager who loved to travel and learn about new cultures. Brown's focus on growth built a sales culture with strong financial controls. He decentralized purchasing, technology, human resources, and other headquarters support functions to each of the 14 divisions and kept the legal, financial, and business-development functions centralized.

Brown's culture of accountability and results has worked with little else in the form of values or mission because of the business Stryker is in—helping people live happier and healthier lives. The end result is meaningful.

But Stryker's system is not for everyone. Over the past five years, Stryker has begun to process-engineer its human resources process to reduce employee turnover. Stryker's overall employee turnover is 14 percent, with most occurring in the first two years. At the director level and above, turnover is 3 percent, perhaps because Stryker promotes from within on over 70 percent of its management promotions. It is a culture of letting your actions speak for you.

What is interesting about Stryker is how well its system works for the company and how logically consistent it is. From an organizational design viewpoint,

1. Stryker has one specific goal—20 percent annual growth.
2. It has a clear behavioral standard—do not lie, cheat, or steal.
3. It gives people responsibility and holds them accountable.

4.   It measures, promotes, and rewards based on re-
     sults.
5.   It recruits high achievers from humble back-
     grounds.
6.   It evolves yearly.
7.   It is customer-centric.
8.   As its operating divisions grow, they are split into
     smaller divisions to create more "ownership" en-
     trepreneurs and positions for promotion.

Most of Stryker's organic growth has come from top-
line growth—it has significant cost-efficiency opportunities.

In January 2005, John Brown retired as CEO, but he
remains chairman of the company and the fourth largest
stockholder. Brown moved his office offsite and is seen
rarely at corporate headquarters because he is committed
to giving his successor, Steve MacMillan, the room to run
his own show.

Stryker has come a long way, but as one would expect,
it faces challenges going forward. Stryker's challenges include

- Maintaining its 20 percent goal and strategy as it
  grows larger.

- Providing the talent the company needs to lead that
  growth. Almost all of its top leaders are in their
  mid-50s.

- How its new CEO will put his imprint on the
  Stryker culture.

- Sustaining John Brown's servant-leadership philosophy, which has prevented leadership hubris, arrogance, and imperial trappings.

- Bringing Stryker's relentless focus and discipline to bear on its cost structure and supply chain.

- Becoming more collaborative across divisions and groups to better serve customers.

John Brown named Steve MacMillan his successor in 2003, handing him the reins of president. Brown explained that Steve's first year here was "my" year, his second year was "our" year, and his third year was "his" year. Steve MacMillan's challenge is to evolve Stryker as it meets new challenges. He is focusing on four initiatives:

1. Globalization
2. Innovation
3. People development
4. Leveraging across the company divisions

Stryker stands for the proposition that you can build a very successful company the old-fashioned way. Stryker stands for moderation, simplicity, humbleness, and a strong work ethic. And it is evidence that companies can grow at significant rates over significant periods of time primarily through organic growth.

Stryker exemplifies a simple, easy-to-understand business model and a small-company soul in a big corporate body.

GROWTH QUESTIONS

1. Can you describe your business in an elevator pitch?
2. Can your employees explain the business and why their job is important?
3. How does your company generate organic growth?
4. Does your company focus on big initiatives—innovations—or on iterative and incremental change?
5. Does your company have a multifaceted strategy or a simple strategy?
6. What drives your growth?
7. How do you drive the top line?
8. Are you best-of-class in productivity?
9. What top-line organic growth initiatives do you have under way?
10. What cost-efficiency initiatives are you undertaking?
11. What productivity initiatives do you have under way?

5

INSTILL A "SMALL-COMPANY SOUL" INTO A "BIG-COMPANY BODY"

HIGH ORGANIC GROWTH PERFORMERS have a small-company soul housed in a big-company body. A small-company soul is entrepreneurial, with employees having ownership of the customer, being held accountable for results, and sharing in the rewards of those results. Entrepreneurial employees are like entrepreneurs—they are energized and engaged in the day-to-day business because they feel that they have some control over their destiny—they have autonomy and respect—and they feel rewarded for their efforts.

These high-performance companies manage this entrepreneurial environment with strong central controls over the backoffice, quality, and financial controls. These controls are evidenced by sophisticated, frequent, and transparent measurement systems that measure much more than financial results. These companies measure operational behaviors that are critical to driving their business models. Many companies talk about giving employees ownership of the customer, but what these companies do very well is manage the tensions between entrepreneurial freedom and the need for standardization and consistent quality, execution, and centralized control. The *organic growth index* (OGI) companies are constantly tweaking the balance between the small-company soul and the big-company controls.

Many employees have the same need for autonomy, respect, and control over their work lives as entrepreneurs. When you ask entrepreneurs why they left a big company, common answers are

"I wanted more control."

"I got tired of being told how to do everything."

"I did not like my boss."

"I wanted to share in the results of my hard work."

"I wanted to do it my way."

"I knew I could do it better than they were letting me do it."

"I did not want to spend all my time working for them and then get laid off."

"I wanted to serve my customers, and they bogged me down in bureaucracy."

"I had different ways of serving my customers, and they would not let me try them."

What these high organic growth companies have learned to do is to create a positive entrepreneurial environment that meets employees' basic needs, and as a result, they have high employee engagement and consistent high performance. In addition, these companies continuously structure themselves to create more entrepreneurial units either by location or by product line so as to create this entrepreneurial environment.

DRIVE RESPONSIBILITY DOWN TO CUSTOMER CONTACT POINTS

Building these types of internal models is a total systems challenge. There is no one silver bullet. It requires a seamless, internally consistent, self-reinforcing system that links culture, structure, execution processes, measurements, and rewards, which all drive ownership of the customer down to the customer-contact level and high entrepreneurial employee engagement.

STRYKER

Let's look at one example—Stryker Corporation, a worldwide leader in the sale of hip, knee, and spine replacements and other orthopedic surgery equipment and supplies. It has a workforce of 16,000 people and a management team that is mostly home grown.

Stryker has hit its goal of 20 percent annual growth 27 of the last 28 years and produced more than 120 employee millionaires. It has very low employee turnover and consistent high performance. Why? Stryker, over a period of years, drove responsibility for customer satisfaction down to the lowest levels—to the levels closest to the customer—through role-modeling and design.

It begins with John Brown's Monday morning meetings with his direct reports to review the prior week's results and to flush out issues of execution and production. To prepare for these meetings, his direct reports met on the preceding Friday with their direct reports, who, in turn, got input from those in the field, those on the factory floor, and those in direct contact with customers in order to know about customer issues, quality issues, competitor issues. Every Stryker factory worker sees a report each day on the prior day's production and quality.

Each Stryker sales person has complete authority to meet his or her customer needs. Many Stryker sales people frequently spend time in operating rooms learning what the doctors want and need. The company sets the target, and its people decide how to execute, earning rewards based on the results they generate.

SYSCO
SYSCO is the largest wholesale food distribution business in the United States. Years ago, it adopted the service profit chain model developed by Harvard Professors Heskett, Sassel, and Schlesinger, which, in its simplest form, states that satisfied employees will create satisfied customers, which will create profits.

The company has 157 separate operating units, with each unit having complete control of its "front-of-the-house activities—marketing and customer-related initiatives"—whereas corporate headquarters has complete control of the "back-of-the-house activities—accounting, money, quality controls, etc." The operating units basically run their own show. SYSCO understands that authorizing every employee to take care of his or her customers—making them *their* customers—changes the whole dynamic.

In fact, the company discovered through intensive research that customer-contact sales people and truck drivers are the key value creators in the company's relationships with its customers. It is the truck drivers who are responsible for delivering more than 400,000 products to more than 100,000 customers a day and who have the most contact with customers. Consequently, in recognition of their important role, the company recently instituted a weekly bonus plan for truck drivers to reward them for efficient and timely delivery of its products.

Similarly, the company used to lease its truck fleet. No more. It found that when truck drivers used company-owned trucks, they took better care of them and kept them looking nicer than if the trucks were rented. This "ownership" mentality is key. When a SYSCO operating unit gets too big, it is split into two smaller entrepreneurial units to maintain that sense of ownership. Stryker does this, too.

SYSCO drives ownership of the customer down to the sales person level. Each sales person visits his or her customer an average of three times a week. The sales people develop friendships with their customers, who usually are chefs or food establishment owners, and they feel a sense of responsibility to help them succeed, going so far as to bus tables or wait on customers if the need arises. The bond is strong.

Many companies espouse the concept that "our employees are owners of the customer" or "our employees serve our customers like they were their own." But the concept of ownership is more than words. To make it work, you need four critical components:

1.   Employee authority and flexibility to do the job
2.   Employee accountability for the job
3.   Variable rewards linked closely to job performance, which is measured frequently
4.   An entrepreneurial be-better (constant-improvement) culture

This responsibility, accountability, measurement, reward, and entrepreneurial culture creates an intensity, focus, and energy level that is habit-forming. As Rick Schneiders says, "If we can link rewards to performance often and in proximate time, our people will see and share in the results of their hard work and want to work harder tomorrow, etc. It is a self-reinforcing system."

Not all the 22 companies are as entrepreneurial as SYSCO or Stryker, but many are evolving. Let's look at Best Buy, which is undertaking a big shift from centralization to decentralization, entrepreneurial store by entrepreneurial store, to a customer solutions company.

BEST BUY
In its infancy, Best Buy was a true entrepreneurial company. As it "replicuted" (replicated and executed) its expansion rollout, however, it became very centralized and headquarters-driven. Store managers had little leeway— there was a company way, and that was it. Now, having established a strong geographic footprint, the company has realized that it runs the risk of losing what made it

work—that entrepreneurial spirit, that customer focus. The solution is to change.

Best Buy is in the process of making its store managers and salesforce owners of their store—"owners" of their customers. They have a new focus: helping individual customers meet their specific individual needs, with the authority to fashion individualized solutions for them— not just push products. Bed Bath & Beyond has a similar policy of the store manager "owning" his or her store, to the point of being able to order his or her own merchandise.

OUTBACK STEAKHOUSE

Another entrepreneurial company is Outback Steakhouse, which was founded by four people who were tired of working for other people and not sharing in the financial rewards. Thus, after starting the business, they made each Outback manager and joint-venture partner buy into the restaurant for a small cash payment—each manager owns 10 percent of his or her restaurant and shares in the annual cash flow from operations and equity buildup. Waiters and waitresses share, too, in a restaurant bonus pool.

As in the case of SYSCO and Stryker, corporate Outback keeps control of the supply chain, quality, and financial activities, but the manager/owner has complete control over the front of the house.

Outback also takes steps to make its large company feel like a small company by creating small units where teams have a "family" feeling, with everyone accountable to everyone else. This small-company feel, or soul, also applies to executives, who act like entrepreneurs. They are hands-on, just like everyone else. They work hand in hand with the employees. They get their "boots dirty" and "eat with the troops." Richard Schulze, founder of Best Buy, also says it this way: "There are not two sets of rules at Best Buy—one for us [executives] and one for them [employees]. Everybody plays by the same rules."

FREQUENT FEEDBACK

Clearly, having an entrepreneurial ownership mentality and a culture that drives responsibility and accountability down the organization chart is beneficial. But what is required to make it all work is frequent feedback.

Employees need constant feedback on how they are doing for two reasons. First, it keeps the intensity and focus level high. Second, it keeps little mistakes from becoming big mistakes. Entrepreneurial organizations know, understand, and expect mistakes. They are a given. And this is one of the major differences between small-company thinking and big-company thinking.

In entrepreneurial companies, mistakes are opportunities to improve. Opportunities to improve fuel a "be-better-each-day" entrepreneurial culture. As Outback states, "Teach not Punish."

A SMALL-COMPANY SOUL

If your goal is an energized work force, you need more intensity, more focus, and better daily execution. Following in the footsteps of the OGI winners requires that

- You must give ownership—authority, responsibility, and power to execute—to those closest to the customer.

- Ownership must link responsibility, accountability, and rewards.

- Feedback based on measurements must be frequent.

- Rewards have to be linked to performance and to be proximate in time to the rewarded behavior.

- You need an entrepreneurial, be-better-each-day culture.

- You need to hire people who have an achievement spirit, who enjoy the challenge of trying to be better each day.

- The closer you can link emotional and financial rewards to the specific behavior, the more you reinforce that behavior.

- You should structure your company into smaller entrepreneurial units.

- Your leadership must live by the same rules as the employees.

Although a goal, this small-company soul and entrepreneurial spirit is not an end state at most of these companies. The OGI winners are constantly trying to figure out how to get more employee engagement—more emotional engagement—from their people. American Eagle, ADP, Best Buy, TSYS, SYSCO, Stryker, Tiffany, Wal-Mart, and Harley-Davidson all have initiatives in place to achieve even more employee engagement.

THE BENEFITS OF A SMALL-COMPANY SOUL

The six keys to organic growth are linked and, to be effective, have to become part of a seamless, consistent, self-reinforcing system. Consistent organic growth requires a systems approach to designing one's strategy, culture, structure, accountability and reward systems, and operational and people processes.

Being entrepreneurial and having the soul of a small company is linked to

- High employee loyalty

- High employee productivity

- Employee stock ownership

- Employee career paths

- Promote-from-within policies

- Senior management teams with long company tenures

- Corporate macro stability

If employees are confident and trust that the "big stuff" is stable and consistent—the business, the strategy, and the stability of management—they can embrace and engage in a be-better, entrepreneurial, evolutionary culture that requires frequent change and improvement. Real employee engagement requires "peace of mind," or trust that the fundamental rules of the game and the key players will not be changed to the employees' detriment.

THE OUTBACK STEAKHOUSE STORY: "THE POWER OF OWNERSHIP"

Outback Steakhouse, Inc., began as one restaurant in 1988. Today, it operates eight different casual dining concepts through 1,100 restaurants with more than 80,000 employees generating more than $3 billion in revenue.

Outback's "Recipe for Success" includes preparing high-quality food from scratch every day and treating its people and customers as individuals to ensure that the company "succeeds one restaurant and one person at a time."

But Outback is not a restaurant company—it is a company of restaurants. Big difference. It operates more than 880 Outback Steakhouse restaurants, more than 160 Carrabba's Italian Grills, more than 60 Bonefish Grills, more than 30 Flemings Restaurants, more than 15 Roy's Hawaiian Fresh Cuisine Restaurants, 10 Cheeseburger in Paradise Restaurants, 2 Paul Lees Chinese Kitchens, and 2 Lee Roy Salmon family restaurants. Understanding that each restaurant is a key point of customer contact forces Outback and its partners to be people-focused. Each restaurant is a separate business unit with a unique ownership.

The founders were two corporate guys and two art majors who had been "ski bums" and had migrated to the restaurant business because of their love for food, on one hand, and, in the other, because of the belief that a business should be able to make money, be fun, and treat people right. Together, Chris Sullivan, Bob Basham, Tim Gannon, and Trudy Cooper had modest goals: Let's own four or five restaurants and earn $250,000 a piece, have fun, and play a lot of golf. Seventeen years later, Outback is a public company, and each founder is very wealthy. More important, they built a business that stands for more than just making money and selling good food.

The company was established because two of the founders felt they were not treated fairly by their former employer, Pillsbury, which owned the Bennigan's chain. Sullivan and Basham were flown to a Pillsbury board meeting to be honored and rewarded for doing an out-standing job at growing the Bennigan's chain and were given an envelope by the chairman as their reward—an envelope that contained an option for a small number of Pillsbury shares. Within four months, both were gone, re-solving that if they were ever to own a business, they would never make anyone feel the way they were made to feel—underappreciated and underrewarded.

This was the underlying motivation behind the unique Outback ownership structure, which requires that each restaurant manager invest $25,000 in his or her restaurant in exchange for a 10 percent ownership stake.

Although Outback's original reason for being was to create a company that did not take advantage of its em-ployees but that shared the benefits of success with those who made it happen, the company became known for much more. Its focus on quality ingredients, made from scratch, fresh, daily; its focus on serving a customer's food the way he or she wants it; its focus on work-family balance; and its focus on being a good corporate citizen made Outback an early adopter of corporate social re-sponsibility.

OPERATING MODEL

Outback was designed to be a dinner restaurant, and the company selects locations close to where people live—not work—which usually results in substantially lower real estate costs. "Dinner only" also means that employees can have some semblance of a family life; in addition, dinners produce higher tips for wait staff than lunch or breakfast would.

Sullivan and Basham also knew the steak business, and over beers one night, the founders dreamed up the Aussie steakhouse image based on the Aussie reputation for having fun despite the fact that none of the founders had ever been to Australia.

Food had to be high quality: fresh, made-from-scratch daily soups, sauces, salad dressings, vegetables, and desserts. Good people serving good food to other good people was the concept.

The restaurant business is a tough one because one bad experience can eradicate three or four great customer experiences, the industry has high employee turnover, and it is very hard to turn out consistent quality every night. In the end, the key is the people. And Outback's founders understood people. They knew that

- People want to be part of something that they can believe in and be proud of.

- People want to be respected, treated fairly, recognized, and have the opportunity to advance.

- People want to have control over their destiny.

To this end, they created the Outback culture, which puts people first—an adaptation of the service value chain in which engaged, happy employees create happy customers, and profits follow.

The company has grown primarily through geographic expansion. Interestingly, except for Outback, the company is not a restaurant concept innovator—it "buys" entrepreneurial concepts and gives their founders a platform, capital, and support to expand, which is how the company acquired Carrabba Italian Grill, Fleming, Roy's, and its new Chinese concept.

OWNERSHIP

Each restaurant is a separate entity owned by Outback, a regional partner, and the restaurant's general manager. Ownership means actual equity ownership—sharing in annual profits and building equity under a buyout formula of five times the last two years' average annual cash flow. In addition, ownership means ownership through stock options.

Other store personnel share in a bonus system on a quarterly and annual basis. In addition, each store has a promote-from-within policy, with a 95 percent track record.

People can see career paths and actual ownership at Outback, where the founders take great pride in the fact that

"We have created more millionaires than any other restaurant company."
"We help people to achieve their dreams."

Outback's culture is one of accountability with respect: "Tough on results, but kind on people"; "No rules—just right."; "We want to be a company of goodness—to our guests, to our employees, and to our communities."

The company is entrepreneurial at the point of customer contact. Each manager/owner and joint-venture partner hires and trains their own people, yet the back of the house is engineered-processed and executes to company standards. The results are lower-than-industry-average employee turnover, sharing of financial results, "ownership" at the customer-contact points, career paths, more employee engagement, promotions from within, and better execution.

At the corporate level, Outback created a company that its people could be proud of. For example, during Hurricane Katrina, in Biloxi, Mississippi, Outback tents with food and water were up and operational before most of the first responders arrived. After 9/11, it erected a mobile restaurant and served hot food to rescuers at the World Trade Center site. It ships its people and food on military transports every year to cook dinners for thousands of U.S. troops in Afghanistan and Iraq. For one trip, 15 Outbackers took more than 6,700 steaks, 30,000 shrimp, and 3,000 giant onions—and for dessert, cheesecake—to feed the troops. The Outback Trust also was established to help employees in need.

ORGANIC GROWTH

The DNA of Outback is a people-first, entrepreneurial, execution culture. It is an inspiring company—an example of how leaders can stay true to their beliefs and values even after becoming wealthy and how treating people fairly still can be consistent with accountability, high standards, and making money.

GROWTH QUESTIONS

1. In your company, what authority or responsibility do the customer-contact people really have?
2. Does your company have an entrepreneurial spirit?
3. Can you feel the intensity? The focus? Is it fun and invigorating?
4. Are people in your company energized and emotionally engaged, or do they just do their job?
5. Do you feel like an "owner"?
6. Do you have control over your destiny?
7. Do you receive frequent feedback other than annual reviews?
8. Are mistakes accepted or punished in your company?
9. Are you rewarded based on your performance?
10. Do you trust your company's system?
11. Are your rules of the game constantly changing?
12. How many change initiatives have you experienced in the last five years?

C H A P T E R

MEASURE
EVERYTHING

ONE OF THE SIX KEYS TO BUILDING A CONSISTENT high organic growth company is measurement—of everything. The 22 companies on the *organic growth index* (OGI) list track a variety of metrics—financial, operational, and behavioral—to understand which areas of their businesses are not performing as efficiently as possible, and then they take action to shore up those numbers. Without measurements, though, they have no way to gauge performance. The right metrics must be in place for both employee accountability and driving the right value-creating behaviors. Operational and behavioral metrics make accountability more transparent, fair, and objective and are mission-critical to long-term organic growth. These companies are, in general, "measurement maniacs."

Sam Walton, for example, was a stickler for numbers

when he started Wal-Mart. He required managers to be in the field Monday through Thursday. Friday was retail merchandising review day, and Saturday morning was financial metric review day. In his autobiography, Walton wrote that he awakened very early every Saturday morning to go over the numbers on every store so that he could discuss them at the Saturday morning manager meeting. Financial metrics helped him to manage the company by identifying opportunities for improvement.

Of course, every public company is required to report financial results to the Securities and Exchange Commission (SEC) and/or to the relevant stock exchanges. This is a given. But great organic growth companies do much more than just measure financial results. They measure every part of their value chain, which has been broken down into detailed parts through an engineering process. They measure, for example,

People behaviors

↓

Detailed customer metrics

↓

Logistic/distribution-chain metrics

↓

Supply-chain metrics

↓

Customer-satisfaction metrics

↓

Quality metrics

↓

Basic financial metrics

MEASUREMENT MANIACS

A common theme running through many of these companies is the extent to which they are internally process-focused. Many of these companies appear to spend as much time on getting the internal stuff right as they do on market-facing processes. This internal focus involves engineering the value chain, technology-enabling the value chain for efficiencies and productivity, and designing extensive measurement systems. I call these companies "measurement maniacs" because they not only measure a lot of different results, but they also do so frequently—daily or weekly in most cases—and their measurement systems are understood by their employees and are transparent. Companies that are world-class measurement companies include SYSCO, Best Buy, Walgreen, Stryker, Gentex, and PACCAR. Let's look at a few examples.

SYSCO

Wholesale food distributor SYSCO works in a low-margin industry, so it has to be efficient. It has to perform at a 99 percent quality level every day, or it will lose money.

To be sure that the company is running well, SYSCO measures 800-plus metrics each week on every operating unit. Then, every Wednesday morning, the top 10 executives meet to review the results with a first pass-through, looking at 20 key metrics for each of its 157 operating units. Variances from plan and the bottom 10 percent of performers are the first focus; then the top 10 percent are canvassed for new best practices, which are disseminated to sister companies.

SYSCO constantly asks itself whether it is measuring the right things. What behaviors produce the most value added? The company measures fuel efficiency and uses sophisticated route-delivery technology to plan delivery schedules. The company measures inventory management, customer penetration, and profitability per customer. Although the company manages thousands of SKUs every day for thousands of customers, it knows that volume per delivery stop is its most critical measure. Selling more stuff to existing customers has a greater impact on the bottom line than anything else.

BEST BUY

"Category killer" Best Buy operates more than 900 stores across the United States and Canada, selling electronics components and accessories for the home and office. Its reliance on measurement as a key to growth began more than 10 years ago.

Best Buy is now providing its retail store managers with in-depth financial training so that they understand store return on investment (ROI) and can recognize which customer segment produces the most profit—not sales, but profit.

Each store manager receives 30 operational metrics daily. They are coded either green (good), yellow (caution), or red (problem). Managers are coached on how to eliminate red problems and mitigate yellows.

The company has spent years studying who its best customers are—learning that 40 percent of its profits come from 10 percent of its customers—and which customer segments really produce profits. The result is the creation of five key customer segments named

- Jane
- Buzz
- Barry
- Ray
- Jill

These customer segments are profiled in great detail, and store sales people are trained to identify, qualify, and meet those individual needs. Darren Jackson, CFO of Best Buy, states: "We use technology and measurements to manage a store's portfolio and business outcome. If we have a fault, it is that we may measure too much. The key is figuring out what to measure and doing the right things with those numbers."

Best Buy (like Walgreen) is seeking to custom fit each store to its customer base.

CHIEF METRICS OFFICER

One of the ways that high-growth companies communicate the importance of continuous measurement is by assigning the chief financial officer (CFO) additional responsibilities related to financial, operational, customer, and people metrics. The role of CFO becomes more of a chief metrics officer (CMO).

The CMO works with senior management and technology enablers to produce the different types of metrics needed to manage a dynamic, growing business. The CMO's responsibility is broader and more operational than that of a traditional CFO.

In addition to Darren Jackson at Best Buy, another good example of a CMO is Laura Weil, former CFO of

American Eagle Outfitters, who recently was chief operations officer (COO) of Ann Taylor. Weil spent her last five
years at American Eagle building a 60-person technology
group that put into place supply-chain, distribution and
logistics, design and production, and store operational
metric systems that are state of the art for the retail industry.

Metrics at American Eagle have focused people on
creating efficiencies. Even though they are five years into
this technology-enabled measurement initiative, each
store manager now receives hourly metrics on traffic,
conversion rates, projected labor needs, and which items
were sold without complements so that store personnel
can be given almost instantaneous feedback on how to increase sales volume per customer.

These companies move along the measurement index
from the simple to the complex, from supply chain to customer relationship management to human resources
management, but they keep improving on what they
have done already. The work in this area is never done.

This attitude permeates most of these companies, and
it is a valuable intangible asset.

TRANSPARENCY OF METRICS/USE OF METRICS

For metrics to be useful, they must be transparent, real-
time, widely disseminated in the business, and used not
only for accountability and teaching but also for rewards.
Most of these companies have learned that measurements can motivate the right behaviors if they are understood, frequent, transparent, and tied to rewards. *Measurements linked with rewards produce the right behaviors.*

Each morning, each manufacturing plant at Stryker Corporation posts its metrics for the prior day so that every employee knows where his or her shift stands on a day-by-day and cumulative basis. Providing timely feedback to its employees allows the company to adjust its behavior to address any deficiencies—a near-real-time adjustment with near-instantaneous results.

Another "measurement maniac" is PACCAR. PACCAR manufactures, distributes, and finances medium- and heavy-duty trucks under the brand names of Peterbilt, Kenworth, DAF, and Leland, although it defines itself not as a truck company but as a technology company.

PACCAR manages and measures quality, costs, efficiencies, productivity, for its 8,800 customers, dealers, and suppliers through technology-enabled information systems from a central command center. PACCAR's measurement methodology is critical to measuring manufacturing flow and is behind 4,000 Six Sigma improvement projects.

FREQUENT MEASUREMENTS HIGHLIGHT MISTAKES AND PROBLEMS

Most high organic growth companies first pick "the low-hanging fruit" and then grow by becoming more cost efficient and productive. But you cannot become more efficient and productive unless you build technology and measurement expertise.

Measurements must be frequent and can be used to monitor problems and keep mistakes small. They not only highlight problems but also illuminate outstanding performance to be shared across the organization, to be rewarded, and to be celebrated.

MEASURING PEOPLE

Interestingly, individual behavior and the use of metrics to drive human resources (HR) processes seem to be the last area that companies focus on for two reasons. First, the study of human resources is less advanced and more difficult to undertake. And second, the importance of human resources in the corporate world has started rising only recently.

Having recognized the importance of HR measurements, some of the high organic growth companies now use the Gallup Organization to assess employee satisfaction and to evaluate candidate hiring strengths and position fit. Stryker even outsources recruitment interviewing to Gallup.

More and more companies are reengineering the hiring process to look at individual personality/cultural fit and competency fit based on internal studies of their best long-term performers. And they know the critical time period during which people are more likely to leave, so management knows when to focus its attention. For Walgreen's retail employees, the critical period is the first year. For Stryker, the critical year is year three.

Because they have integrated the six keys to organic growth into their operating models, the 22 growth champions generally have very high employee satisfaction, high employee loyalty and productivity, and employee turnover substantially below industry averages.

MEASUREMENT/TECHNOLOGY/ENGINEERING PROCESS

The measurement process and level of sophistication are directly related to obtaining specific behaviors or results. Without measurement, you have no way of knowing who is performing above or below expectations, and you can't address any deficiencies. Measurement and engineering process go hand in hand with being an execution champion, which is built on a foundation of world-class technology and technology people. How you integrate technology people into your business is an important variable.

In many companies, information technology (IT) workers are "people over there who do not understand the business." But there is another way.

American Eagle, for example, imbeds its technology people into the different functional areas, with the chief of technology overseeing the function and IT employees. Imbedding helps the technology people—60 at American Eagle—to understand the operational issues and gives them a greater sense of being part of the team instead of being just a service provider.

Best Buy, on the other hand, outsources its entire technology function to Accenture. Either way, the key points are

- Focus on measurements.
- Enable measurements through technology.
- Use engineering process to illuminate what to measure.
- Measurements must be frequent.
- Measurements must be transparent.

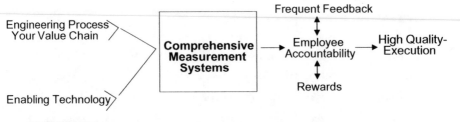

FIGURE 6.1
COMPREHENSIVE MEASUREMENT SYSTEMS.

- Measurements must affect rewards.

- Measurement excellence is an ongoing process.

- CFOs are migrating to be CMOs.

- Measurements illuminate variances, mistakes, and problems.

A comprehensive measurement system (Figure 6.1) is as key to being a consistent organic growth company as having a simple business model and an entrepreneurial culture and structure. It is this measurement system that implements the necessary linkages and self-reinforcing nature of the six keys.

YOU NEVER GET IT RIGHT

Although high-growth companies are constantly improving, they never, never reach the end state. They are never satisfied with the level of success they have attained. They keep working at execution, employee engagement, and measuring operational behaviors.

Great organic growth companies are a blend of farmer and software engineer. Like farmers, they get up each day, till the soil, fertilize, weed, water, harvest, and re-plant. And like software engineers, they incrementally improve, they iterate, they test, they prototype and beta test, and they keep improving every part of their value chain. And they use measurements to determine their progress on a daily basis.

THE BEST BUY STORY: "HOW TO KEEP A SUCCESSFUL COMPANY ENGAGED"

When you walk into a Best Buy store, what do you sense or feel? Energy. The place is alive—there is an intensity in the air. Best Buy's corporate headquarters, in a suburb of Minneapolis, consists of four office buildings connected and accessed through a central concourse, like an airline terminal's spoke-and-hub system. It has a grand atrium where its amenities are located: the highest-grossing Caribou Coffee store in the United States, a large dining area with different food stations, the Best Buy shop, a health care and fitness facility, a day-care facility, a dry cleaning and laundry dropoff, and a set of conference rooms.

More than 4,000 employees go through this area to and from work every day, and it is filled with energy. The flow of people, the smiling faces of friends or acquaintances, and the impromptu work meetings that congregate on the side energize the place.

Best Buy is a company designed down to the smallest detail for energy, interaction, and collaboration. Every officer or manager office is small—very small—and windowless because the company wants its officers out of their offices. The CEO's office is the same small size, windowless, although he has an adjacent conference room just big enough for a round table and four chairs for small meetings. The rest of the employees can make use of hundreds of breakout rooms, conference areas, and community areas within the buildings for meetings, discussions, and problem solving.

Founded in 1977 by Richard Schulze as an audio stereo equipment store, the company has grown to become the largest specialty retailer of name-brand consumer home entertainment and home office electronics equipment. Best Buy has more than 600 stores under the Best Buy name, 100-plus Future Shops in Canada, more than 20 Magnolia Audio Video Stores, and the Geek Squad—a computer and digital service repair and consulting group.

As a stand-alone big box retailer, Best Buy currently has about a 15 percent market share, with stores ranging from 15,000 to 43,000 square feet. The company employs more than 110,000 people. Its revenue base of more than $27 billion is made up of

Consumer electronics	37%
Home office	37%
Entertainment software	20%
Appliances	6%

Since 2000, Best Buy has grown revenues 18 percent a year and net income 23 percent a year. It currently operates in the United States and Canada and is in the process of expanding into China.

Best Buy's corporate culture is defined by four values:

1.   "Have fun while being the best."
2.   "Learn from challenges and change."
3.   "Show respect, humility, and integrity."
4.   "Unleash the power of our people."

The company defines its core competencies as "World-class in store experiences, customer orientation, inventory management, and merchandising."

Its organic growth story has followed a traditional path: Open more customer locations fast, take market share from the competition, and then focus on operating costs and efficiencies. Best Buy does what it does very well.

It can open stores efficiently and in the right locations. It uses technology to manage inventory selection, the supply chain, logistics, and merchandising and is leading edge in customer analysis, data mining, and customer segmentation. The company manages its stores by focusing on maximizing per-square-foot profit of its floor space. Best Buy is not trying to beat the discounters by selling commoditized products. Instead, it sells value-added products that allow the company to make its margins while operating efficiently to generate an exceptional return on invested capital. In other words, Best Buy is a very good operating machine.

HISTORY

Best Buy has divided its almost 40-year history into five eras:

1966–1971	Humble beginning
1972–1982	Growth and challenges

(continued)

1983–1990	Forging new paths
1991–1999	Unprecedented growth
2000–present	Reaching new heights

Humble beginnings began in 1966 when Richard Schulze and a business partner opened a Sound of Music store in St. Paul, Minnesota, that grossed $173,000 its first year. They bought two companies during the next year and opened two more Sound of Music stores. In 1969, the company went public as an over-the-counter stock, and by 1970, revenues had reached $1 million.

The growth and challenges era began in 1972 with expansion, new facilities, new products, and establishment of seven more stores. In 1981, a tornado hit the Rockville, Minnesota, store, and Schulze had a "Tornado Sale," introducing the idea of low prices in a "no frills" retail environment. The company continued to expand with photography products, TVs, video equipment, and home office technology.

Notice Best Buy's organic growth trajectory: first, more locations; second, more products; and third, no frills—reduced costs. The third era brought a new name—Best Buy—and the opening of its first superstore. In 1985, Best Buy raised $8 million on NASDAQ through an initial public offering (IPO) to fund the opening of three more superstores. A 12-store expansion was financed by a $33.6 million stock offering later that year. And in 1989, Best Buy changed its format again to offer customers pressure-free, noncommissioned sales personnel in a warehouse-style store and adopted the yellow tag logo.

Geographic growth outside of Minnesota began in

1991 in Texas and Chicago, and in 1995, Best Buy implemented its major technology operating platform.

The reaching new heights era began in 2000 with Best Buy acquiring Magnolia Hi-Fi, a high-end retailer, to add a new customer segment, and in 2001, it expanded to Canada when it bought Future Shop, Ltd. In 2002, Best Buy bought the Geek Squad, another small-concept acquisition.

After achieving a 10-year compound annual earnings growth rate of 34 percent, how does Best Buy plan to continue its organic growth?

- First, Best Buy is decentralizing its structure to become more entrepreneurial at the store level by adopting a customer-centricity service and merchandising model.

- It will continue to expand at a rate of 60 to 70 stores a year in the United States and Canada until it reaches 1,200 stores.

- It is experimenting with a new 20,000-square-foot format to saturate existing markets.

- It is experimenting with three new focused concepts in Chicago.

- It will increase efficiencies further by expanding direct sourcing and reengineering the supply chain.

- It is reengineering its customer-contact centers.

- It will create more exclusive entertainment content.

- It will upgrade and renovate existing stores.

- It will align and revamp its employee policies to affirm and motivate the new customer-centric decentralized model.

CULTURE

Most changes at Best Buy, whether moving from commissioned to noncommissioned salespeople or changing to a large-box format, were done to make the shopping experience better for customers. "Best Buy earns its business one customer at a time," says Richard Schulze, chairman and founder.

And the Best Buy culture of servant-leaders is illustrated by CEO Brad Anderson's turning down stock options during the past three years and having them put into a pool for Best Buy employees.

CUSTOMER-CENTRICITY

Best Buy's biggest shift to date has been its shift to a decentralized model (each store is a separate business, like Outback) where the store manager has more control over his or her store, and employees are trained to solve specific customer issues instead of just selling products.

Customer-centricity—that is, the customer is the central focus—grew out of Best Buy's economic value-added (EVA) analysis of customer segments and its decision to make capital decisions, inventory mix, and format size governed by the profitability of the portfolio of customers. Instead of managing traffic, conversion, and revenue, store managers are being trained to optimize a customer portfolio and business outcome.

This customer-segmentation approach has led Best Buy to create a customer model based on five customer prototypes:

The affluent professional
The younger male who wants the latest gizmo

The family man and practical buyer

The suburban mom who wants products to enrich her kids' lives

Small-business customers

All this has the objective of identifying the right customers—the profitable ones—and becoming closer to them so that they are more likely to spend more at Best Buy during their lifetime. Best Buy is now putting in as much focus on the science of customer segmentation and customer data mining as it has historically on its supply chain and its technology operating platform.

NEW GEOGRAPHY/CONCEPTS/FORMATS

In addition to expanding beyond North America into China, Best Buy also will open smaller stores in certain markets to saturate them (as Wal-Mart and Walgreen have done). It is testing three new "studio" stores: Studio D, which targets women customers; Escape, targeting the young urban male professional, and EQ-life, a home-health concept. All three of these new concepts are in the test phase and are being done completely outside Best Buy to allow them to be totally unhampered by Best Buy assumptions (just like IRIDESSE at Tiffany & Company and Martin & OS at American Eagle Outfitters).

HUMAN RESOURCES

Best Buy is also putting an intense focus on becoming a talent company. To this end, it is revamping its rewards systems to better enhance and mirror its values and culture, as well as its new customer-solution model. The Best Buy culture is being modified to treat customers as "Kings and Queens" and the employees closest to the customer as "Royalty," with headquarters employees being "Servant Leaders."

With the help of the Gallup Organization, Best Buy has adopted the employee strengths concept and is becoming more scientific in recruiting for "FIT"—managing employee careers to play to their strengths and helping people "*find their inner flame*," according to Randy Ross, vice president of human resources.

Just as marketing has drilled down to segment customers according to their needs, HR has implemented an ambitious plan to segment employees into five different groups based on what matters most to them or draws them to be engaged at a consistently level of high performance. Different training, different rewards, and different work environments for those five employee segments may come out of this initiative.

Best Buy has had a policy of promoting from within—about 50 percent of its store managers come from within, and more than 75 percent of promotions above store management are filled from within. This, added to the fact that 75 percent of full-time employees own stock in the company, demonstrates that as in supply-chain, merchandising, and customer management, Best Buy continues to drill down to get better and to "capture" the energy and passion of its people. Given its culture of humility, where arrogance is not accepted, you have a company that is trying to treat employees as royalty. The absence of corporate jets and executive perks and the small, windowless offices for everyone remind the leadership that it is not about them or because of them—it's about the customer and the employees.

To illustrate further, as a learning tool, here's what a few of the company's key executives have to say:

Our mission as leaders is to put in place something that will live on—be sustainable. It is a constant battle of paradoxes; entrepreneurial vs. bureaucracy; fighting complacency and self-satisfaction which results from success; and to keep rejuvenating the core business and to look for new geographics or concepts for the future. Managers have to live our values—20 percent of their annual option grant is dependent upon whether they walk the talk. If you want to work at Best Buy—leave your ego at the doorstep.

Al Lenzmeier, vice chairman

We are a very energized company, but we have to be even better at getting people focused on getting the right results. Wouldn't it be great if we could help every employee at Best Buy find his or her passion and give them opportunities, which excite them and energize them even more.

Randy Ross, vice president of human resources

Best Buy's single-most watched metric is employee engagement. Because we find that when employee engagement is up, so is our profitability, so is our customer satisfaction, so is our bottom line.

Darren Jackson, CFO

At Best Buy, technology is an agent of change. Every business process has been mapped onto BOB (Business Operating Blueprint) and all are being changed to fit new best-of-breed technologies in order to create more transparency, reduce costs, and increase efficiencies.

Bob Willet, EVP operations and CTO

Best Buy stands out as one of the most energizing, inspiring, and uplifting places around. The company does not know what is next, but it does know that to be the best, it needs engaged people who are open to continuous change and experimentation.

The experiment continues. Just this last October Best Buy announced a refocus on employee engagement, a major initiative to improve store personnel retention even further, and a major overhaul of its technology system to allow for the customization of individual stores by customer and product segments.

GROWTH QUESTIONS

1. What behaviors are you measuring?
2. What are the key value drivers that you measure?
3. What do you do with your measurements?
4. What measurements are given daily or weekly to line employees? Do they understand why you focus on these specific measurements?
5. How do measurements affect salary differentiation or bonuses?
6. Do your line employees understand the three or four key measurements to which they contribute?
7. How do you use measurements to enhance employee engagement?
8. How do you use measurements to enhance employee "ownership" of the customer?
9. How do you use measurements to drive the right behaviors?

BUILD A PEOPLE PIPELINE

LL THE HIGH-GROWTH COMPANIES HAVE HIGH MANAGEMENT and employee retention, high employee loyalty, and high employee productivity as compared with their competition. Most of these companies also have high employee stock ownership. Together, they form the people pipeline—a deep bench of committed, engaged employees from which to build a management team. And the *organic growth index* (OGI) winners certainly have deep bench strength. The average tenure of employees at TSYS, for example, is seven years. Seventy-six percent of Wal-Mart store managers started in hourly positions. Tiffany promotes from within 70 percent of the time. Best Buy's employee turnover is 20 percent below the industry average, although its goal is to be 50 percent lower. And SYSCO's human capital index measures employee loyalty and productivity.

The 22 organic growth companies have leadership teams with more than 20 years' average tenure. Sixty-five percent of SYSCO's 46,000 employees, 50 percent of ADP's employees, and 75 percent of TSYS's employees own stock in the company. The average tenure of a Walgreen store manager is 13 years, and ADP has 90 percent associate retention.

These companies have a deep bench of engaged employees—people who have bought into a system in a committed way—a key competitive advantage. You lose time and effectiveness when you have to train new employees continuously. If you have high turnover, it is hard to build a be-better entrepreneurial culture. The opposite of employee turnover is an engaged workforce. An engaged workforce is focused, committed, and continuously trying to be better, with a financial and emotional stake in the outcome. Engaged employees take responsibility for and ownership of their jobs, are held accountable for their results, and share fairly in the rewards. And they know that if they play by the "rules of the game" and work hard, they can advance, have a career, and maintain a long-term position with the company. This type of system produces higher levels of engagement.

EMPLOYEE ENGAGEMENT IS KEY

Despite having different types of corporate cultures—from employee-centric to customer-centric to results-centric—high organic growth companies create environments that foster consistent high performance, high

employee loyalty, and employee engagement. Some succeed without even having a vision or mission statement.
Some have mixed-message cultures. Some companies put
a lot of focus on culture (TSYS), whereas others have operated for years with an unwritten one (Stryker). Some
companies have a people-centric or employee-centric culture, which focuses first and foremost on taking care of
employees. Companies such as TSYS, Outback, ADP, and
Walgreen try to create a team or "family" environment,
which builds loyalty to the team and the obligation to
work hard and not let your teammates down.

Harley-Davidson, Tiffany, Waters, and American Eagle have a culture based on excellence and quality of the
product. The product is the focus. Stryker and Wal-Mart,
on the other hand, are results-oriented. And SYSCO has
a service-profit-chain culture that says that satisfied employees will create satisfied, loyal customers and thus
profits. TSYS and Outback adhere to this philosophy, too.

Interestingly enough, whether the focus is on the employee, the customer, the service-value chain, the results,
or the product, these companies all get to the same place:
an engaged, loyal, highly productive work force.

So what is common across cultures? Or companies?
When you talk to executives and human resources (HR)
executives at these companies, you find some common
themes.

LACK OF AN ELITIST, HIERARCHICAL ATTITUDE

High-growth companies know that sustainable success
depends on line employees, not on the management
team. And because most managers have spent their en-

tire career with the company, coming up through the ranks from line employee to management over the course of 20 or 30 years, they recognize the value of everyone on the team. Managers have not forgotten where they came from. They remember that someone mentored them, gave them a chance, and that the system rewarded their performance.

AVERAGE TENURE OF TOP MANAGEMENT TEAMS

Company	Average Years at Company
Walgreen	33
TSYS	32
Bed Bath & Beyond	25
NVR	23
Best Buy	21
SYSCO	21
Brinker	21
Tiffany	20
NVR	18
Harley-Davidson	17
Waters	16
ADP	16
Outback Steakhouse	15
Stryker	15
Gentex	14

THESE COMPANIES UNDERSTAND PEOPLE

Line employees, in general, want the same things management wants. They want to be treated with respect and dignity, to be listened to, to be valued, to have the opportunity to create a better life for themselves and their families, and to be part of something special. They also want the opportunity to be all they can be—to be given opportunities, to be graded (measured) fairly, and to advance as far as they can go so that they can make a better life for themselves and their families.

There are companies that say that they support these goals, but what makes the high organic growth companies stand out is that they go beyond words to execution:

1. The companies act consistently and in harmony with their policies.
2. There is a seamless linkage across their culture, their HR system, and their measurement, accountability, and reward systems that motivates the desired behaviors and results.

At high-growth companies, there is a high level of trust in the system. Employees see results. They see the promotions from within. The link between performance, results, and rewards is clear to them. What kills employee engagement and loyalty is lack of trust arising from the failure of management either to act in harmony with the rules or to play by the same rules.

AN IMPLIED SOCIAL CONTRACT

There is an implied social contract between a high-growth company and its employees that the rules of the game will not change midstream and that if you play by the rules, you will have a job with advancement potential. Employees work hard for companies where they believe they have a future and where they can have an impact. And when they see that current top managers started out where they are now, as line employees, a powerful, self-reinforcing system is created.

But the attitude and resulting behavior of top management is key. Humbleness is mission-critical. Top managers who have a sense of entitlement or superiority generally do not fit at high-growth companies, where humility is more important than status. Top management receives few perks at these companies. For instance, Best Buy and Walgreen have no corporate jets. And most of the OGI winners do not spend lavishly on executive offices. Except for compensation, the companies try to eliminate elitist executive perks.

SYSCO

Years ago, SYSCO adopted the *service-profit-chain model*, which states that satisfied employees produce satisfied, loyal customers, which produce profits. Using this model, SYSCO has implemented policies that have generated industry-high retention rates and employee satisfaction. SYSCO has made a science of measuring these results, and the difference the company has found between operating results with high employee satisfaction and those with low employee satisfaction is significant.

SYSCO SERVICE-PROFIT CHAIN

	Work Climate Average	Operating Pretax Percent	Operating Expense as a Percent of Sales	Workers' Comp Percent of Sales	MA Retention	Delivery Retention	Associates per 100,000 Cases
Top 25% work climate	4.01	7.5%	13.3	0.07	85	88	4.13
Bottom 25% work climate	3.61	5.3%	14.9	0.20	72	78	4.33
Variance	0.40	2.2%	1.6%	0.13	13	10	0.20

DIVISIONS WITH HIGHLY SATISFIED ASSOCIATES
DELIVER BETTER RESULTS

At SYSCO, it is clear that satisfied employees are more productive at a lower operating cost. Look at the retention rate of the company's people pipeline.

SYSCO (2004)

Level	Retention Rate	Average Tenure (years)	Average Age (years)
Executive Vice President & Above	100%	22	55
Senior Vice President	100%	26	54
President	97%	23	51
OPCO Executive Vice President	98%	20	48
Specialty MIP	93%	21	49
Corporate Vice President	100%	20	52
Corporate AVP	93%	12	48

TSYS

TSYS is the second largest credit-card processor in the United States and has high employee retention and productivity owing in good measure to its people-first culture. Its "Culture of the Heart" espouses that if you take care of your employees, good financial results will follow. It follows through on this policy with a promote-from-within mandate and an employee wealth-building program.

The executives at TSYS have spent between 21 and 40 years at the company and its parent organization, where they have been trained to be "servant leaders," serving, coaching, and helping employees to serve customers.

TSYS shares the rewards of its success with its employees through a four-component wealth-building plan that allows employees with one or more years of service to buy stock four different ways. Through these programs, more than 75 percent of TSYS employees have become actual owners of the company. Under three of the programs, TSYS can contribute up to 7 percent of salary to each of the three employee stock-purchase programs, and under the fourth program, the company matches employee stock purchases 50 cents for each employee dollar invested up to 7 percent of compensation. In recent years, TSYS has contributed 11 percent of employee compensation to employee stock-purchase programs.

TSYS has doubled its employee base every $3\frac{1}{2}$ years while growing more than 20 percent a year for the 20-year period from 1983–2003. As Rick Ussery, retiring CEO, states, "There are four important groups: (1) employees, (2) shareholders, (3) customers, and (4) vendors. And my job was to make them all feel like they were number 1."

ADP

ADP is one of the largest front- and backoffice administrative outsourcing companies, now worth $86 billion. ADP never has forgotten its roots, however. Founded by three sons of immigrant textile-mill workers who believed in the American dream, the owners made sure that all of their associates could purchase stock under its stock-purchase plan when ADP went public in 1961. In part, because of this, ADP has high employee retention and employee stock ownership.

WALGREEN

Walgreen historically has hired people from small towns in the Midwest with a great work ethic. This attitude of humbleness has distinctly shaped the company's corporate culture. Its executives fly commercial airlines, not corporate jets, and there are no assigned parking spaces for senior management. Offices are the same size for everyone from the director level to the CEO, and the company prides itself on its open-door policy—anyone can see the CEO.

At Walgreen, everyone from the top down demonstrates a commitment to and respect for the company's people. In the early 2000s, a young Walgreen executive was diagnosed with colon cancer. Walgreen's president told the employee that he could keep his job as long as he wanted but to focus on getting well. During his treatment, Walgreen executives routinely visited him at home, and the CEO called his wife frequently. And when the young executive died, Walgreen people turned out in droves for the funeral because a "family member" had passed away.

Similarly, at TSYS, employees stepped in to help care for a midlevel employee with cancer who was quite sick. On their own initiative, employees took turns bringing cooked dinners for her and her family every day for months until she recovered. When one of the team needs help, fellow teammates help at TSYS.

WAL-MART

Now Wal-Mart is an interesting case. On the one hand, it promotes from within, it has an aggressive diversity program and a world-class diversity training program, and it pays full-time people well above minimum wage. On the other hand, it has a large sex-discrimination class-action lawsuit against it, lawsuits over "working off the clock," and issues in California, Maryland, and Georgia concerning health care coverage.

Wal-Mart's culture, which emphasizes treating each employee with respect and dignity, is reflected in its very diverse team. Of its 14 board members, one is female, two are African-Americans, and two are Hispanic. Fifty-nine percent of its workforce are female, and 30 percent are minority. Females hold 40 percent and minorities hold 20 percent of management positions.

From the store-manager level on up, it has high employee retention and a promote-from-within policy. And with 1,700,000 employees, it gets consistent high performance.

OUTBACK STEAKHOUSE

What sets Outback apart from many other restaurants is its concept of employee ownership. When two of its four founders quit Pillsbury and partnered with two others to create a new restaurant concept, they were motivated to create a company that shared the rewards with employees who contributed to the company's success. As a result, they built a great business with high employee satisfaction and low employee turnover.

Every restaurant manager, joint-venture or regional partner, and in some cases, chefs, too, are required to invest $25,000 to $50,000 cash for a 6 to 10 percent ownership interest in the restaurant depending on the concept. Store managers then are paid a base salary, and they receive stock options and 10 percent of the restaurant's profits. They have a five-year employment agreement, and at the end of five years, they can resign or sell back their ownership interest based on a formula of five times the average cash flow for the last two years. Most managers who work at Outback for 10 years become millionaires. They also care about their restaurant, act like owners (because they are), and are able to engage their employees.

Interestingly, Outback has no HR department. Regional or district partners and store managers are responsible for hiring and training their own people, with help from headquarters. As Outback has grown, it has promoted people from within and given employees opportunities to own part of "their own" restaurant as they expanded. In addition, each restaurant has a profit-sharing program for waiters, waitresses, hosts and hostesses that is paid out quarterly.

IT ALL FITS TOGETHER

Based on these case studies and what you know about high organic growth businesses, what would you do if you wanted to build a great company? You might consider some of the following principles shared by top performers:

- The people doing the work need to understand the business and the importance of their individual jobs, as well as how their success will be measured and what is important to the success of the business.

- Everyone has to buy into a system of accountability and a culture of constant improvement.

- Only by giving employees "ownership" of their jobs can a company truly have a constant-improvement culture that works.

- People need constant, reliable, and objective feedback in order to learn and improve. To correct mistakes, they need real-time metrics. And metrics require technology.

- Great execution depends on the linkage of accountability, measurement, and reward systems, as well as on a stable, engaged workforce.

- A stable, engaged workforce results from a stable macroenvironment; an implied "social contract"; home-grown, humble operators as leaders; the devaluation of elitist perks; the fair sharing of the results; and promotion-from-within policies.

- Growth continues because of a relentless focus on all aspects of the value chain and because of deepening relationships with customers.

THE TSYS STORY: "A CULTURE OF THE HEART"

TSYS is the second largest credit-card processing company in the world, with revenues of $1.2 billion and more than 5,000 employees. It is a sophisticated technology-based company that developed several state-of-the-art software systems to service payment and customer processing for credit-card issuers. Its clients include Provident, Capital One, MBNA, ABN AMRO of the Netherlands, JP Morgan Chase & Co., Bank of Ireland, and Pitney Bowes, among others.

If you asked any high-level business or technology executive how to build a world-class software company, they likely would advise you to build it near a technology or educational center such as Boston, Austin, Palo Alto, Washington, DC, Research Triangle, or near an IBM plant in Boca Raton or Boulder. The common wisdom held that to build a great software company, you need the best technology, talent, and engineers from the best schools, and you need to hire managers with great software backgrounds, all of which are readily available in these technology hubs.

But this is not the route TSYS took when it set up shop. TSYS opted to build a high-performance technology company in a small town near the Alabama state line, relying mainly on home-grown talent without ties to a major educational or technology employment base. And the company succeeded.

TSYS's success can be described as the power of ordinary people doing extraordinary things together. TSYS began as the credit-card processing department of a small Columbus, Georgia, bank—CB&T—in 1959. In 1973, CB&T began processing credit cards for other banks and grew from there.

The company's chairman was one of the founders of the processing department at CB&T 40 years ago, and the company's CEO began at CB&T in 1974. Its president has been there 25 years, and other senior managers have tenures ranging from 21 to 35 years. Yet none of its executives are engineers or software designers by education.

The company has been able to create a work environment that engages its employees to successfully compete internationally as a technology solutions provider to major financial institutions and businesses without top technology graduates from major universities.

How did the company do it? TSYS was built on a culture of servant leadership. Executives serve employees, and employees serve customers. And taking this one step further, employees learn how to serve customers based on how they are treated by their managers and leaders.

TSYS'S CULTURE*

Synovus Financial Corporation (the successor of CB&T) is an $8 billion market-cap community bank holding company created in 1888 that owns 81 percent of TSYS. TSYS actually was spun off by Synovus in 1983. Since almost all of TSYS's senior executives originally came from Synovus, the Synovus culture carried over to TSYS.

CB&T started in the credit-card business in 1959, handling all the processing manually. In 1966, the company bought its first computer. At the time, IBM had checking-account software, but no company had yet created credit-card processing software. Therefore, without any training in software, engineering, or computers, Rick Ussery and two others wrote the first software to process credit cards.

During the early 1980s, the company's growth created a significant need for TSYS computer programmers. TSYS responded not by recruiting on college campuses nationwide but by partnering with Columbus State College to create a software engineering program to train high-tech

---

*Adapted from Drazin, Hess, and Mihoubi, "Synovus: 'Just Take Care of Your People,' " in Hess and Cameron, eds., *Leading with Values: Positivity, Virtue and High Performance* (New York: Cambridge University Press, 2006).

workers. Over the next 10 years, TSYS hired more than 2,000 people from the program.

TSYS created a solution for its most pressing need—people—solving its own problem like it solves customer problems. The company also long ago adopted a promote-from-within policy that, along with its culture and employee wealth-building program, has led to high employee loyalty, satisfaction, and high retention among its technical workforce.

Over the years, TSYS found that for its bright, young people, the risk of losing someone peaks in the third year, and thus the company created a program to celebrate and reward people for achieving the third-year anniversary. Magically, the "third-year itch" was minimized.

What employees cared most about was money and their kids. Thus TSYS created a wonderful wealth-building program that now has 75 percent participation. And for the kids, the company built a $4 million state-of-the-art day-care center in its new facility. TSYS treats its employees the way management would want to be treated and receives loyalty and tremendous effort in exchange.

TSYS's culture can be summarized as a blend of the Golden Rule and doing what's right. This means treating others right, with kindness and encouragement. Decision making follows from this, even when *right* may not be the most profitable, the most expedient, or even the most popular avenue. This approach extends to the families of TSYS employees, others that TSYS comes into contact with, and finally, out to the community. There is a sense of building a better family, a better community, and being a part of a better world that TSYS makes possible.

PERFORMANCE COMES SECOND

The value chain begins with people, with performance being necessary, but people first. Performance comes from good people with good values. Management's role is seen as stewardship because the company is seen as an asset borrowed from the shareholders that must be maintained as if it were one's own. A distinctly nonsecular approach to spirituality manifests as a belief in a "higher power," a belief in the inherent worth of every employee, and a commitment to developing the talents of each individual.

The company strives to maintain an atmosphere in which employees grow "materially, spiritually, and intellectually" and where the customer sees that the culture comes "from the heart." At TSYS, there is a deeply embedded commitment to "walk the talk." Some have given this corporate philosophy an almost religious or cultlike status.

In addition, a "family-like" atmosphere permeates the culture, based on the notion that people are valuable. Employee evaluations are not threatening once-yearly encounters but rather ongoing and interactive discussions. Servant leadership, or the notion that management serves the organization, rather than the other way around, translates into management-as-mentor or -coach rather than the traditional boss-subordinate relationship.

This approach translates directly into the company's success because the company aims to follow the axiom that if we "take care of people, profit takes care of itself." It is believed that an employee's life should not be "compartmentalized" into all its component parts but that rather, the office environment should feel similar to all other parts of one's life.

WALK THE TALK

For TSYS, living its values begins with compensating its employees adequately for their commitment and dedication. Employee benefits are grouped under the four broad categories of "health, wealth, well-being, and time." Professional development is also encouraged, with TSYS employees offered the opportunity to enroll in the Columbus State University masters of information technology program.

Living the culture translates directly into superior customer service. In a competitive financial services market, employees "extending" themselves for their customers translates into greater consumer loyalty and higher product sales.

But Synovus also believes strongly in personal accountability. The company maintains

> Our values also describe a company at which every member is fully responsible for every loan, account, market trade, every client and every customer. That's 100 percent responsibility. No excuses when something goes wrong, just make it right. Mediocrity is never a solution. Every member of our team should have zero-tolerance for anything less than the best. That's us; that's our way.

Leaders treat employees like they want the employees to treat customers.

TSYS LEADERSHIP EXPECTATIONS

TSYS works hard at developing its leaders internally. It has a Leadership Institute that puts everyone through a values assessment and creates a leadership-development program for each leader. TSYS stresses the concept of harmony: Think and act in harmony with key beliefs about how people should be treated. Leaders are taught that employees will act as leaders act.

The company asks each manager to

- *Live the values.* Do the right thing, apply the Golden Rule, take 100 percent responsibility, value differences, establish trust, gain credibility, earn respect, demonstrate fairness, walk the talk, and *reach* out and have fun.

- *Share the vision.* Communicate clearly, understand the vision, articulate corporate strategy, align team goals with corporate strategy, and develop an action plan.

- *Manage the business.* Create a team environment, play by the rules, embrace our customer covenant, execute results within budget, create shareholder value, think twice, and serve with high energy.

- *Make others successful.* Practice servant leadership, coach for optimal performance, facilitate individual development, be accessible, create opportunities for team members, and recognize and reward others.

ORGANIC GROWTH STRATEGY

TSYS has grown by incrementally solving customer problems. Solving problems generally required new software solutions, which then were converted into products for use throughout the client base.

TSYS prides itself on customer connectivity, listening to their needs, and responding quickly and professionally. Even with its success, stable cash flow, and thousands of loyal employees who have made a lot of money as stockholders, TSYS still pushes to be better, as illustrated by recent annual goals:

- Improve our "Great Place to Work" ratings.
- Grow revenues by 30 to 33 percent.
- Align resources to support the TSYS growth strategy.
- Maximize productivity by eliminating inefficiencies.
- Embrace our "Customer Comment."
- Increase our net income by 22 to 25 percent.

Rick Ussery, chairman of TSYS, is one of TSYS's founders. He summarizes how TSYS was built:

> We were all young in 1983, and we believed nothing is impossible, it just might take a little longer. Our culture was simple—follow the Golden Rule. Leadership's role was to make the four key groups—employees, customers, shareholders, and vendors—feel like each was number 1. As we grew, we tried to be a big company with a small-company mentality.

Phil Thomlinson, the CEO, has been with TSYS and its predecessor for 30 years:

> We built a company based on customer service. We look for employees with a caregiver mentality like a nurse or a teacher mentality. We have little company

politics—we are more like a caring family—TSYS cares for you—you care for TSYS. Of the people who leave us for more money, over 60 percent want to come back to this environment. We can not ever become satisfied. We have over 100 get better initiatives. We have to, as leaders, stay accessible. I have an "Ask Phil" program. Any employee can call or e-mail me and ask anything confidentially. I get 15 to 20 a week. We represent opportunity for our people—over 60 percent of management are female; 30 percent are minority.

An example of the opportunity for growth is Colleen Keynard, who started 35 years ago as a file clerk and today is an executive vice president, having run all our operations, and is now in charge of our largest account.

TSYS is successful because TSYS is a multitude of individual success stories.

Opportunity, a caring culture, caring for the customer and each other, and sharing the wealth all have worked for TSYS. Every TSYS employee who has been with the company for one year qualifies for four wealth-building plans in which the company can contribute up to 21 percent of the person's salary to stock purchases, depending on company results, and a stock-purchase plan where the company will match 50 cents for every employee dollar to purchase stock up to 7 percent of the employee's salary, depending on source and pay.

TSYS stands for the proposition that if you engage your employees in a mission of excellence and align your culture, rewards, and actions, it is amazing what people can accomplish.

GROWTH QUESTIONS

1. What do your employee satisfaction ratings show?
2. What are your employee turnover and retention rates?
3. What is your turnover in customer-contact positions?
4. What does it cost you to lose an employee?
5. Do you have a promotion-from-within policy?
6. What percent of your positions are filled by promotions from within?
7. What is the average company tenure at your top levels?
8. What is your management team's attitude about employees?
9. Do you have a deep bench of experienced managers?
10. Do you have a succession plan in place for every key leadership and management position?
11. What percent of your employees own stock in your company?

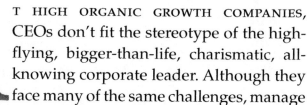

LEADERS: HUMBLE, PASSIONATE, FOCUSED OPERATORS

A
T HIGH ORGANIC GROWTH COMPANIES, CEOs don't fit the stereotype of the high-flying, bigger-than-life, charismatic, all-knowing corporate leader. Although they face many of the same challenges, manage thousands and tens of thousands or, in one case, millions, of employees, and struggle to maintain their competitive edge just as in any major company, this group of leaders is very different.

Rather than being overly confident about their success, at high organic growth companies, leaders are frequently paranoid about complacency, arrogance, and hubris. Although many leaders are very wealthy, for the most part, you would not know this from their dress, their office, their demeanor, their attitude, or any outward appearance. They are also very willing to give credit to others, often stating that the sole reason the company is successful is because of its employees, not because of the officers or the leadership team. Few of the leaders, if any, take the credit themselves. There is a sincere respect for line workers, where many had begun their careers. Many have personal stories about their humble beginnings. All understand deeply the fact that it is line employees who serve customers one transaction at a time.

In discussions with them, almost all reflected on past times that were very difficult—how they or the company had tough times. A lot of credit for their success was attributed to being in a growth industry, to luck, to their employees, to their mentors, and to being in the right place at the right time rather than owing to their brilliance.

High-growth leaders do not assume that they know all the answers. There is a belief in trial and error, testing, iteration, and "Gee—we ended up differently than we expected," as well as the sense that they and the company cannot stand still or stay the same and continue to be successful.

None claim to be the best, although their performance is obviously superior to that of their peers.

THE VALUE OF HUMILITY

Let's look at the leaders of some of the companies studied in some detail. Notice the similarities across industries. Notice the surprising, refreshing humility. These leaders are centered and comfortable inside themselves and work hard at leading in a way that reinforces the growth system that many have built over the years.

AMERICAN EAGLE OUTFITTERS

American Eagle's executive offices are located in a suburb of Pittsburgh in front of a large warehouse distribution center. The space is nice but small and definitely not
what one would call opulent. CEO Jim O'Donnell has
been at American Eagle six years, formerly having been
chief operations officer (COO) at the GAP. He has spent
most of his career in the retail industry and does not have
an MBA.

O'Donnell is an operator, not a salesman, and he is
very into the details of how to stay close to his customer
base of 15- to 25-year-olds. He's also committed to using
technology to gain more efficiencies in the design of
clothing and on-the-floor times for merchandise. He con-
cerns himself with the details of shopping-center leases,
store designs, keeping the culture "on the edge," and focusing on continuous improvement.

Roger Markfield is vice chairman and chief merchandiser at American Eagle and a 23-year veteran of the company. He is the keeper of the culture, the man who knows
everyone in the office and warehouse by name.

He is the outward "people guy," whereas O'Donnell's
focus is on operations—being better each day. No one at
American Eagle is "full of themselves" or takes success
for granted. Markfield starts each morning by turning on
his computer at home, looking at the previous day's store
results. This team is into the details of the business. They
understand the difficulty of staying successful, having
seen many retailers fail during their 30 to 40 years in the
business.

Both of American Eagle's leaders are humble and
open men who talk freely about past mistakes and cur-

rent challenges. In my interviews with them, both sought to learn from the other companies I studied. They recognized their weaknesses and were proud that they had "partners" that brought strengths to the table that covered for those weaknesses. Both were very focused and into the details of the daily operations for which they were responsible. They were engaged in the minutia of their business. Markfield took me on a tour of the distribution warehouse and addressed each employee, asking him or her how his or her day was going and inspecting the merchandise, giving praise, and acknowledging to me, in front of them, how important their jobs were. There was no air of authority or regality, just teamwork.

BEST BUY

All executive offices at Best Buy are the same size, all barely big enough for a desk and two chairs. Every executive office except for Dick Schulze's, the founder and chairman, is an inside windowless office, including the CEO's. Windows are for team spaces—a higher priority than management.

Schulze is now retired and serves as chairman. He is a billionaire, having benefited greatly from his founding of Best Buy, but he takes no credit for that accomplishment. Instead, he says, "Employees were the center of the company, and for Best Buy to stay good, every employee had to feel part of, and be included in, the Best Buy process. Best Buy had to provide opportunities for its people to grow. People had to have the opportunity to contribute and achieve and succeed and move up"

Although Best Buy is its industry's leader and has produced significant growth results for years, the company is still focused on better employee engagement at the store level and at the point of customer contact. Best Buy has not been happy with its store-level employee retention rate and with the emotional engagement of store-level employees, so the delivery model had to change.

The challenge is to change a great marketing operation into a great retail operation, and the company cannot do this unless it works harder to include every line employee. Fortunately, the leadership at Best Buy has to have the same rules and accountability to employees as the employees do to the leadership, which goes a long way toward attracting loyalty and buy-in. "At Best Buy, there are not two sets of rules, one for us and one for them. There is one set of rules for all of us," says Schulze.

Al Lenzmeier, vice chairman of Best Buy, has worked there for 25 years. He is a former CFO and has spent much of his time recently on the China initiative. He created the Best Buy Leadership Institute and also concentrates on "how we treat people" and "our values." His focus is on stewardship and sustainability—how they can ensure that Best Buy "can live on." He said that this goal requires a constant vigilance focused on

1.   "The tension between entrepreneurship and bureaucracy,
2.   Not getting complacent, and
3.   Institutionalizing reinvention as part of our DNA."

Lenzmeier says, "We have to make each store feel like a small company—so [that] each employee feels part of the company with input and the ability to try things." How do you sustain your values? Your culture? At Best

Buy, 20 percent of every senior executive's annual option grant depends on his or her living the company values with his or her team. Every member of the leadership team has a personal coach.

Every leader I interviewed at Best Buy was focused on the line employees in the store. Many, including CEO Brad Anderson, had long tenures at Best Buy, starting at the store employee level. They have not forgotten what it is like to be there, and they know their continued success depends on those employees executing at consistent high levels of quality. The entire leadership mentality at Best Buy is evidenced by its CEO refusing stock options recently and asking the board instead to place them in a trust for the headquarters employees. His behavior stated, "I have enough. I do not need more. I am well paid." Refreshing.

TSYS

Phil Tomlinson, the current CEO, joined the company 22 years ago from GE and helped to build the company on service—one satisfied client at a time. According to Tomlinson, "Leaders serve employees, and employees serve clients. Leaders take care of employees, and employees take care of clients." Tomlinson works hard at keeping himself and his team humble, believing that "the downfall of many a CEO is when he takes that first step onto his new corporate jet."

You have to stay humble. You cannot let pride be your downfall. You have to constantly challenge, be open, and learn from others. He said that they constantly ask themselves, "What's the right thing to do? And the right thing may not be the best legal or financial answer."

WAL-MART

Lee Scott, the CEO of Wal-Mart, has talked in a March 2004 NPR interview about the Wal-Mart culture and the fact that associates are more important than executives. He calls the "Open Door" program, whereby employees can contact the CEO about anything they're not satisfied with, the "life blood of our linkage with our associates."

He also relates a story about the truck drivers who went to Sam Walton and asked him to fire Scott. Walton brought Scott over to his office and asked him if he thought he could change, and he said, "Yes sir, I think I can." And then Walton had Scott thank each one of those truck drivers for having the courage to use the open door. Had they not done that, had Scott not changed, he would not have the CEO job now. He says, "I've had Open Door issues this week from individual associates, from managers, and in the last few months, I've hired back a terminated associate because I didn't think it was right they were terminated. I think our associates have representation in people like myself."

In a January 2003 *Financial Times* article, Scott reported:

> Our culture is not an intellectual culture, you've probably noticed that. Our culture is an emotional culture. I had a guy in here the other day, he's been here just a few months. Very smart guy. And he had told somebody after he'd been here two weeks, I understand the culture. I'm ready to go. I'm ready to move forward. Intellectually, I bet he does. But it isn't something that can be intellectualized. It is a feeling.
>
> This kid was in here last week from Aurora, Missouri; he's been a department manager for us for 20 years. I said, "What kind of problems are you having?"

He said, "I'm not getting the merchandise I need." I said "What do you mean?" He said, "Let me give you an example. We had an item that they didn't send us because we're a small store. And I was looking at the sheet to see what was selling in other stores. So I called up and got them to send me 24, and we sold eight in the first week." He'll sell all of them. . . .

Sam always said there are only two people he would not give a second chance to: anyone, management or hourly associate, who stole, or a manager who abused their people. I believe that rigidness; you have to have it. This company rides on the back of the store people and the distribution people. This is not a company that is out there looking for the next strategy that is going to take us to the next 10 years, where the CEO is the most important person in the company because they have to understand technology, and they're going to bet the capital on the newest drug or the newest electronics item. That's not the way this company works. This company works for the store, and the distribution centers, up. And the hardest thing for new people to get into their mind is that you come in here, you're now a senior vice president of Wal-Mart stores, you walk in that door, and the first thing you have to learn is you're not terribly important. And it is more likely, if there's two people standing in the hallway and they both need to talk, in this company it is most likely that the hourly associate is going to be talked to first, and you're going to wait until they're finished before you get your turn. And I want to tell you, we think it's natural; it is a hoot to watch new people as they struggle!

TIFFANY & COMPANY

The image of luxury jeweler Tiffany & Co., based in New York City, fashion capital of the United States, is based on power and wealth. Yet Mike Kowalski, CEO of Tiffany, and Jim Quinn, president of Tiffany, are just like the other CEOs: humble operators—not full of themselves—no trappings of power—but focused on doing their job. Mike's mantra—"Growth without compromise"—is his focus. Mike attributed his success at Tiffany to "being dealt a good hand," and his "job was not to mess it up." The pervasive theme was to grow the company without sacrificing quality, the brand, the culture, or the legacy. He took pride that Tiffany, while being a luxury jewelry store, had no doorman and no locked door to keep people out.

Jim Quinn is similar. When asked to describe the Tiffany culture in one word, he said, "Humility. There is only one star here, and it is Tiffany."

STRYKER

John Brown, the chairman of Stryker Corporation, built a very successful company and became a billionaire himself in the process. Even with all that success, Brown did not change. He still lives in the home he bought in 1977, only recently trading his old Mercury Sable for a new one.

Brown is a quiet, humble man who learned in 1982 that he could not "run a growing company with an iron fist," nor be the central and controlling figure at Stryker if it was going to grow. He learned to delegate, to decentralize, and to give people the opportunity to grow, prove themselves, and prosper.

Brown built a company on a simple strategy—"Grow 20 percent a year"—and on a simple code of conduct—

"Do not lie, cheat, or steal." Brown's simplistic policies worked for him. He stated, "Strategy is not the key. All you need is a good strategy with *great* execution."

Brown always stressed that how we treat people counts more than what we say. He was a proponent of "Speak softly" and let your actions speak for you. In his view, the great leaders are servant leaders who do not lose sight of what is important.

FIGHT ARROGANCE AND HUBRIS

These companies acknowledge that it is difficult to resist taking success for granted—to fight arrogance, to fight self-satisfaction, and to fight the trappings of power. The companies' leaders often express their understanding that success can be fleeting:

> OUTBACK: "You are only one bad meal away from losing hundreds of customers."
> AMERICAN EAGLE: "We are only two floorsets away from disaster."
> SYSCO: "We are only as good as our last delivery."
> SYSCO: "With a 16 percent market share, 84 percent of the people must think we are not that good."
> BEST BUY: "At Best Buy, failure is not an option; being paranoid is part of our DNA."
> TSYS: "Many a CEO's downfall begins when he takes that first step on his new corporate jet."
> WALGREEN: "Arrogant people and people who treat other people badly are not Walgreen people."

WHERE ARE THE HARVARD MBAS?

Of the 22 current and 8 former CEOs who are now chairmen of the companies in my study, only three have MBAs. Surprising? Not really.

What we have learned from these companies is that the essence of business is the ability to relate to, communicate with, and engage on a deep cognitive and emotional level with employees and customers. Business is done through and with people. People skills, emotional skills, communication skills, and empathy are all business skills that leaders and managers can learn on the job and from different educational and life experiences. In fact, most business schools do not teach these skills. They teach analytical tools, theories, models, and rules but not interpersonal skills.

In fact, having an MBA can be a hindrance—because MBA training may suggest that principles, theories, and models are more important than people. And if you do not develop the ability to communicate with, care about, connect with, and engage people in the quest for execution excellence one customer, one transaction at a time, all the training in the world may not matter. You will have difficulty generating organic growth.

We have also learned that these companies are great execution companies and that their leaders are mostly great operators. They have learned how to manage execution processes and how to drill down through engineering process to focus on the details that matter—again, skills not taught in most MBA programs. The leaders of the companies we studied, in general, focus on a few basic leadership principles, such as "take care of your people," "eat with the troops," the Golden Rule, and leading by example. They understand that hypocrisy and hubris can kill their execution entrepreneurial cultures. And they work hard at staying in the front lines of their businesses with the people who really count—their employees.

THE TIFFANY STORY: "GROWTH WITHOUT COMPROMISE"

Tiffany & Co. is an interesting story for several reasons. First, Tiffany is one of the oldest of the 22 companies, having been founded in 1837 by Charles L. Tiffany. It has mostly prospered during the last 168 years, which is an accomplishment in itself given that the average lifespan of a major corporation today is less than 40 years.

The second interesting fact is that Tiffany stayed true to its founder's vision of creating and selling fine goods to its customers in the famous Tiffany "blue box," which was introduced in the 1800s. No, the "blue box" is not a recent Madison Avenue creation; it, too, has survived more than 100 years.

Part of the reason for Tiffany's longevity and success has a lot to do with its leadership, which exhibits an understated passion, respect, and reverence for what Tiffany stands for. Despite the company's luxury brand and upscale image, the company leaders are far from arrogant or highbrow. Instead, they are thoughtful, down-to-earth, focused, humble people who are grateful for the opportunity to try to preserve and enhance the Tiffany brand during their tenure. In demeanor, the Tiffany executive team is no different from the SYSCO or Best Buy team—

focused, humble leaders deeply engaged in the details of executing the business.

HISTORY

Tiffany is a company rich in history, steeped in the design and creation of fine products made with diamonds, platinum, gold, and silver. Tiffany was the first U.S. company to use the 925/1000 sterling standard, which became the U.S. standard, and the company's designers actually created the current seal of the United States on the dollar bill. In 1885, Tiffany introduced "Audubon," its top selling silver flatware, and in 1886, it introduced the world-famous "Tiffany setting"—the six-pronged diamond solitaire engagement ring. Tiffany created the Super Bowl and World Series trophies and is the oldest and longest current daily advertiser in the *New York Times.*

In 1940, Tiffany moved to its Fifth Avenue flagship location, which today produces more than $200 million in revenue and sales of more than $5,000 per selling square foot.

Tiffany sells more than $2.2 billion of fine objects through approximately 155 stores located in the United States, Japan, Europe, Canada, Central and South America, and Asia/Pacific Rim, as well as through more than 25 million copies of its Tiffany catalogues. It has more than 25 million visitors a year to its North American Web site.

Tiffany's ownership has changed four times: from the Tiffany family to Walter Hoving in 1965, who sold the company to Avon in 1979, who sold the company to management and investors in 1984 for $135 million, and then to public shareholders when the company went public in

1987. In the last 20 years, the value of Tiffany has grown from $135 million to its current market cap of $4.4 billion.

Charles Tiffany, in 1837, set the policy that Tiffany would not negotiate price nor ever have a sale. In fact, in its 168-year history, Tiffany has only had two sales, one in 1955 and one in 1985, to generate quick cash for the leveraged buyout.

More than 80 percent of what Tiffany sells is jewelry, and it creates and manufactures about 80 percent of its products. Tiffany today is a vertically integrated company. It has diamond sourcing contracts with major suppliers, its own in-house design team, its own world-class diamond laboratory, its own cutting and polishing facilities in Belgium and Vietnam, and its own manufacturing facilities in Rhode Island and New York.

U.S. sales represent about 60 percent of the $2.2 billion in annual sales, and Tiffany's base product is fine diamond engagement rings. Tiffany has the highest luxury-brand awareness (over 50 percent) and employs more than 7,000 people, with more than 2,000 working in its retail stores. Tiffany's mission is to "Enrich the lives of its customers by creating enduring objects of extraordinary beauty that will be cherished for generations."

In layperson's terms, Tiffany creates timeless fine jewelry of such a high quality that it can become a family heirloom. Tiffany strives for quality, excellence, and trust, and its customers rely on Tiffany's reputation and credibility.

ORGANIC GROWTH STRATEGY

Tiffany's organic growth story is an annual combination of measured geographic expansion, new-product introductions, value-chain enhancements, and giving customers more reasons to buy Tiffany products. Tiffany grew classically first through store expansion in the United States. Today, Tiffany operates 59 stores, 26 of which are in the top 50 U.S. markets, and the company cautiously and measurably opens four to six new stores a year. After expanding in the United States, Tiffany opened its first store in Europe.

In Europe, Tiffany faced tough competition from other legendary and historical fine jewelry houses, although it had more success in Japan, its largest international foray, which has grown substantially in the last 30 years.

In addition to geographic expansion, Tiffany created new revenue by introducing major new product lines annually in silver, gold, and platinum jewelry. Tiffany's move to be a vertically integrated company in order to protect its brand and its quality has brought Tiffany new profit centers, including diamond cutting, diamond polishing, and manufacturing.

Tiffany then expanded its channels of distribution to the Internet, first in the United States and more recently in Japan, the United Kingdom, and Canada. Then it closed its wholesale business, reduced its business sales offerings, and made two small acquisitions, including The Little Switzerland chain of Caribbean jewelry stores. The company also made three entrepreneurial investments—two in developing new diamond mines in Canada and one in starting a new pearl jewelry chain called IRIDESSE.

Tiffany has invested heavily in technology throughout its value chain in order to operate more efficiently and today is concentrating on customer relationship management to increase revenue.

A WORK IN PROGRESS

Although Tiffany is 168 years old, it is still a work in progress. Over the last five years, it has become a state-of-the-art human resources (HR) company, focusing on developing Tiffany leaders and its management pipeline, as well as a state-of-the-art distribution and logistics company and a technology-enabled engineering process company throughout its supply chain. And today it has major initiatives on customer relationship management and sales training. Tiffany undertook all these initiatives to control its quality and enhance its brand.

The people side of its business is strong, too. Tiffany has exceptionally low turnover for a retail business—less than 10 percent—and Tiffany employees are proud of where they work and proud of what they sell.

The company has evolved to make its sales people more entrepreneurial by giving them the power to "own" and resolve customer issues. Tiffany's senior management team all have at least 15 years' experience at Tiffany, except for the new head of HR, who arrived four years ago. The CEO has been with the company 25 years; the president, 19 years; the CFO, 22 years; the senior vice president of operations and manufacturing, 17 years; and the senior vice president of merchandising, 15 years.

When asked to describe the Tiffany essence, DNA, or culture in one word, the most common words used were

"Humility"

"Pride"

"Passion"

UNIQUENESS

Although Tiffany is a mature company with a finite market for luxury goods, it has set goals of 15 percent return on equity (ROE), 10 percent return on assets (ROA), and high single-digit sales growth. The overriding priority of the Tiffany management team is to preserve and protect the brand, and this means measured growth. Even though the company believes it can accommodate 45 more stores in the United States, it limits new-store growth to a fraction of this annually. Part of the reason for the slower pace is to be able to staff the new location with 50 percent current Tiffany employees and 50 percent from local fine jewelry stores. Tiffany chooses quality over quantity when it comes to fast growth.

CUSTOMER SEGMENTATION

Two years ago, Tiffany did something generally unheard of on Wall Street. It took steps to slow down the growth of entry-level price points in silver jewelry by raising prices. The company was concerned about traffic count, service, delivery, and brand dilution. In effect, it believed that it was selling too much product to a particular market segment and that long term it could hurt the brand. So the company stopped.

At the same time, Tiffany is constantly seeking new reasons for customers to buy to celebrate life's joys or for themselves. Special times should be celebrated with a special self-purchase, the company suggests.

CREATIVITY/ENGINEERING PROCESS

Tiffany is an interesting mix of art (creativity, design, and advertising creativity) and science (engineering process of the supply chain, manufacturing, quality control, and the developing science of customer relationship). The company seeks to connect emotionally with its customers and its employees through the quality of its products.

Every business decision is made with Tiffany's brand image in mind. Tiffany's customers, investors, employees, and the general public expect Tiffany to act in a certain way and not to be associated with or act in ways that tarnish the brand of America's greatest jeweler. The company is clear about its niche and its mission, as evidenced by comments by chairman and CEO, Mike Kowalski: "We have learned that there are a limited number of things we do well, and we have to be focused and disciplined to do those things. We are a products company—not a brand to be licensed or to be affixed to other products. We do not believe that we can sell anything or any luxury item—we know how to create, manufacture, and sell the highest quality, natural gem jewelry in the world. Pure and simple."

HUMBLE, FOCUSED LEADERS

And while being proud of its heritage, Tiffany's leaders are protective of its image. According to Kowalski, "While striving for quality, Tiffany has never been elitist. We always have had democratic stores—no doorman— no locked doors—no determination of who should be allowed inside. We are part of this country's history, and we are an American brand—American made."

Tiffany devalues self-satisfaction, self-promotion, corporate politics, and internal competition. It seeks to be a place that energizes its people to contribute to the tradition, to be part of making history, and to be part of an American icon.

When Tiffany began its quest for operational excellence through technology, it looked outside the retail industry for best-of-class systems. In the last five years, Tiffany has brought the same level of process improvement to its HR area. It implemented a new performance-appraisal system that focuses on competencies and accountability. And it has become more focused on line-employee training and the rewarding of brand-enhancing behavior—personal self-development and cross-functional and collaboration skills are now being taught.

Tiffany's employee satisfaction surveys are outstanding, employee retention is over 90 percent, and it generally promotes from within. It rarely hires a vice president–level candidate from the outside, and at least 50 percent of its managers and 65 percent of its store directors are promotions from within. More than 50 percent of its employees own stock.

EXECUTION OF EXCELLENCE

Whether it is customer data and research, artistic design of advertising, jewelry design, executive management, inventory management, vendor management, or raw materials and diamond testing and ratings, Tiffany strives to be best of class. The Tiffany standard is applied to all phases of its business, not just the design and manufacture of jewelry.

Tiffany manages its product-development and new-design rollouts on an 18-month rolling basis, in a process that Jon King, senior vice president of merchandising, calls an "iterative process; we constantly assess and reassess." His use of the following words shows the intensity, discipline, and emotion of being part of Tiffany: "Here, managing the brand is an excruciating process—the microscopic focus on the details of execution."

BE MORE ENTREPRENEURIAL

Tiffany, like Best Buy, is in the process of instilling more entrepreneurial freedom and responsibility within its sales force. During its 168 years, Tiffany prided itself on being able to say "No"—Tiffany just does not do certain things. However, in trying to improve customer service, the company learned that it was sending away many customers because of its rigid rules, including some of its regulars. Consequently, Tiffany instituted a new company-wide sales training program called "YES: Tiffany Exceptional Service" that calls for sales people to be customer relationship builders, not just product sellers. Sales people now "own" their customer relationships and are fully responsible for customer satisfaction.

Tiffany is trying to become even closer to its customers and to increase conversion rates through focused selling around personal life events. Entrepreneurialism has evolved to where local store managers control their allocation of charitable contribution dollars and client development dollars.

To the credit of its senior management team, its culture, and its history, Tiffany is grounded in and passionately committed to creating the highest-quality products efficiently and in a manner that enhances the integrity of the Tiffany brand.

GROWTH QUESTIONS

1. How much time does your leadership team spend listening to line employees?
2. How much time does your leadership team spend listening to customers?
3. How accessible is your leadership team to any employee?
4. Is every employee inquiry to the leadership team answered promptly and directly?
5. What perks do members of your leadership team enjoy that differentiate them from employees?

BE AN EXECUTION AND TECHNOLOGY CHAMPION

THE HIGH ORGANIC GROWTH COMPANIES GEN-ERALLY do not have unique strategies, products, or services, nor are they market-leading innovators. But they are execution champions—day after day, they have figured out how to get consistent high-quality performance from their people. A critical design in each system is the use of measurements, real-time information, and the technology enablement of the entire value chain. These companies use technology to enhance their productivity and efficiency, which allows them to produce outstanding results that are shared with employees.

Although they are known primarily as specialists in other areas, the *organic growth index* (OGI) winners, especially Wal-Mart, Walgreen, American Eagle, Best Buy, TSYS,

SYSCO, PACCAR, ADP, Gentex, Waters, and Harley-Davidson, also have state-of-the-art technology systems in place. And it's their technology that makes superior execution possible.

Many companies have a simple, easy-to-understand, focused business model. Some have good customer service. Others are the low-cost provider in their market space. Outstanding organic growth companies, though, do *all* these things very, very well. They all

- Are focused and stay focused on their businesses
- Have engaged their employees
- Have an entrepreneurial, be-better environment
- Have seamlessly and consistently aligned accountability and execution processes with measurement and reward systems
- Have engineered and technology-enabled most of their value chain
- Have built a people pipeline

They also have technology in place that facilitates high organic growth. Technology enables information transparency, operational efficiencies, productivity, real-time measurement, feedback, and greater customer knowledge, segmentation, and service. Just look at the use of technology in some of the high-growth companies on our list.

LEVERAGING TECHNOLOGY

To illustrate these points, let us look at a few examples of companies that pride themselves on being technology companies, even though none of them sells hardware or software.

WALGREEN

Walgreen has a tradition of being a technology early adapter. As early as 1981, it linked all its pharmacies by computer, and in 1991, it became one of the first retail chains to introduce point-of-sale scanning. While Walgreen's organic growth model is primarily "replication" of opening stores and saturating markets, its technology prowess allows it to distribute logistically and manage inventory store by store. It is now introducing inventory management by department, allowing each store manager to have access to every other store's inventory information to see what's selling best.

Walgreen continues to enhance its distribution-center technology to further reduce inventory reorder cycles, reduce out-of-stock items, and include on-demand rapid-response reorder systems. Walgreen's next goal, which is the same as Best Buy's, is to customize each store's inventory based more on the demographics of the store's customer base. Customer data mining and demand-based store stocking are the future.

BEST BUY

Best Buy is completely revamping its technology supply-chain and inventory-management systems to take into account its customer-centric initiative so as to have stores within stores to serve specific customer demographics. This means more customized inventory for each store and requires Best Buy to deliver daily profit-and-loss statements (P&Ls) to each store so that each can see the results and learn from specific trial initiatives.

Technology is also driving Best Buy's new customer loyalty system, which has six million frequent high-volume Best Buy customers in it, with specific targeted priority marketing activities in place.

Best Buy, through its China sourcing office, is now using technology for interactive design and manufacture of Best Buy–branded products—mainly customer-demanded accessories. Last, Best Buy is using technology in its human resources function to build a "strengths and desires database" that better fits employees with their desired positions.

WAL-MART

No discussion of execution champions would be complete without Wal-Mart. Because of Wal-Mart's expertise in logistics, supply chain, satellite communications, and inventory management, I am convinced that it probably can sell any product at a cost less than any competitor. Despite a workforce topping 1.7 million employees, the company has not stopped executing.

Wal-Mart was not an early adapter—it took employees years to convince Sam Walton to invest heavily in technology. But when they succeeded, the company focused on logistics and distribution and then financial systems. Wal-Mart continues to evolve technology-wise as it experiments with just-in-time inventory for its stores and new inventory- and merchandise-tracking systems. Wal-Mart's technology prowess includes a technology service center for its stores and a commitment to drive further efficiencies throughout its value chain.

HARLEY-DAVIDSON

Although Harley-Davidson has a respected brand and product and loyal customers, it is its operational excellence that makes it viable, stable, and resilient. It has survived the ups and downs of being sold to AMF, then being repurchased by management, and ultimately going public, and it continues to grow organically at a fast pace.

Harley-Davidson has three simple rules:

1. Know the customer.
2. Take nothing for granted.
3. Never stop learning.

But its technology is what helps to drive productivity and metric tracking. After investing heavily in building technology systems, it turned to its supply chain to efficiently integrate its more than 600 suppliers into the manufacturing process. Technology and execution excellence have allowed Harley-Davidson to keep all its manufacturing operations in the United States.

GENTEX

Gentex has a three-pronged strategy: Execute, execute, and execute. It is the world's leading manufacturer of electrochromatic, automatic-dimming rearview mirrors for the automobile industry—a high-tech computer chip–based product. Each mirror goes through 600 distinct quality tests along 15 automated assembly lines in Michigan, with the results being 99.5 percent error-free quality.

Like Harley-Davidson, Gentex also manufactures all its products in the United States, and they are both market leaders without having to resort to off-shoring or outsourcing.

TIFFANY & COMPANY

Tiffany & Company is well known as America's premier luxury jewelry brand, but what most people do not know is that Tiffany is also a world-class manufacturing and supply-chain company. Tiffany believes that you cannot outsource quality and uses technology to drive efficiencies, productivity, and quality throughout its supply and distribution chains. However, it also controls the quality of its product from source to store through joint-venture ownership and exclusive supply contracts with diamond mines in Canada, to diamond cutting in Vietnam, to diamond polishing and rating. The company is now turning to technology to improve the customer service and human resources functions.

SYSCO

SYSCO is the largest wholesale food distribution company in the United States, selling food products under its own brand name and others, and it owns the supply source of many of its products. SYSCO is a world-class supply-chain and logistics company, and with the opening of its new distribution facilities, it is enhancing its distribution efficiencies even more.

At SYSCO's annual meeting in 2005, the chairman and CEO started to rebrand the company as a supply-chain logistics company. What SYSCO is doing is similar to Wal-Mart's strategy of taking a technology-based, hard-to-imitate world-class competency and leveraging it across products.

SYSCO knows that it must continue to use technology not only to control and manage its 157 operating units but also to drive costs down to allow it to enter new lower-price customer segments without sacrificing industry-leader margins.

AMERICAN EAGLE OUTFITTERS

American Eagle has built a 60-person information technology (IT) team that it has embedded into corporate functions so that the team members understand the operations they are trying to make faster, better, and cheaper. Technology now links a designer's idea of a fashion through the design, costing, bidding, manufacturing, logistics, and distribution process. Such systems are also making American Eagle more efficient in inventory management, overstocks, price optimization, inventory movement, and store operations. Technology is driving improved conversion ratios and making possible the matrixed execution of 10 inventory changes a year in every store.

PACCAR

PACCAR manufactures and distributes medium- and heavy-duty trucks under the names of Peterbilt, Kenworth, Leyland, and DAF, but it calls itself a technology company, not a truck company or a manufacturing company. PACCAR has technology-enabled its entire supply chain, its manufacturing process, and its dealer chain and has built a world-class call center for truckers. It has more than 4,000 Six Sigma improvement projects in process and continuously measures quality metrics, inventory time, and assembly hours. It has the capacity to let each customer build his or her own custom truck as efficiently and as fast as building a standard truck through its use of a robotic assembly. Again, world-class execution of world-class engineering processes enabled by technology.

THE AMERICAN EAGLE OUTFITTERS STORY: "MERGING FASHION AND TECHNOLOGY"

American Eagle Outfitters, based outside Pittsburgh, is focused on selling value-oriented fashion merchandise to 15- to 25-year-olds through its more than 800 retail stores in class A malls and downtown urban areas primarily in the United States and Canada. American Eagle is interesting for two reasons:

1. It has not had stability at the CEO level—having had three different CEOs in the last six years.
2. It is the "Rockie" of the OGI group, having gone through and overcome tough times twice in the last eight years.

Through all of this, it has kept an entrepreneurial spirit and has changed in several significant ways. First, in the past six years, it went outside the company for new high-level design talent. Second, it has become a technology-enabled engineering process company across its design, supply-chain, distribution-chain, and store operations.

American Eagle began in 1977 as an outdoor apparel store—an offshoot of the Silvermans retail chain, owned by the Silverman family. It grew too fast, and in the 1980s, it brought in an outside investor—the Schottenstein family from Columbus, Ohio. Then, in the early 1990s, the Schottensteins, who also own Value City, took full ownership and control. At the time, American Eagle competed based on low price, just like Value City.

In 1994, American Eagle tried unsuccessfully to redefine itself. By 1997, it had found its niche—value-conscious fashion. It operated very successfully in 2000 and 2001 and then lost touch with its customer base and became too trendy—it was too far in front of its customers' tastes. But again, American Eagle righted the ship and had good years in 2004 and 2005.

The company has grown through geographic expansion, but facing geographic saturation, American Eagle announced in late 2005 the creation of a new concept—Martin and Os, a sportswear concept for 25- to 40 year-old customers. Historically, the company has competed by boosting its bottom line through operational and productivity efficiencies, as well as organic growth through Internet sales. It is now remodeling older stores.

American Eagle's mantra now is

- Stay close to the customer.
- Have the best talent.
- Execute.

And the company has done a good job. Among 12- to 19-year-olds, American Eagle is the third coolest brand, after Nike and Sony, and ranks second with that age group, after Old Navy, in shopping penetration.

TECHNOLOGY ENABLEMENT

American Eagle began its operational efficiency program in its design, manufacturing, sourcing, and supply-chain areas first. Then it moved to distribution and inventory management. Now it is focused on store operations, with a goal of driving conversion rates and complementary selling.

OPERATING METRICS

	YTD Sept 2005	YTD Sept 2004
Comparable store sales	+20%	+16%
Transactions per store	+15%	+10%
Average unit retail sale	+ 8%	+ 7%

Its store-opening metrics are very strong. The first 12 months of operating results for 67 new stores opened since January 2003 are

FIRST 12 MONTHS OF OPERATIONS

Average store net sales	$2.12 million
Cash flow	$470,653—22% of sales
Investment	$527,996
Pretax return on investment (ROI)	89%

And look what happens when it remodels stores. For stores remodeled (20) in 2004:

	Pre-Remodeling	Post-Remodeling
Sales	$1.9 million	$2.8 million
Profit	$492,000	$900,000
Profit/foot	$114	$164

So how will American Eagle continue to grow organically? It has a number of opportunities, including

- Continued geographic expansion (40 to 50 new stores in 2006)

- Continue to grow existing store growth 6 percent or greater

- Drive store sales productivity up to $550 to $600 a foot

- Add new products—intimates, personal care, etc.

- Grow American Eagle Direct—the Internet business

The company's goal in taking advantage of these opportunities is double-digit earnings-per-share (EPS) growth.

COMPLEXITY OF EXECUTION

The complexity of American Eagle's business is mind-boggling. The company rolls out six different displays a year, with four additional major changes. The company has to design, source, manufacture, distribute, and have the right merchandise in the right place in every store 10 times a year. Roger Markfield, vice chairman and "chief merchandiser," calls it "putting on 10 Broadway shows a year." Hundreds of SKUs and different colors, all which are managed through technology and the use of a laboratory store in the home office, where layouts and inventory placement plans are finalized for dissemination throughout the chain. And as you can guess, coordination between functions is critical. When you factor in that most of the sales people in the stores are part-time students and store managers around 25 to 26 years of age, achieving outstanding execution is remarkable.

With the fickleness of fashion trends, staying humble is easy—as the CEO Jim O'Donnell stated, "We are only one floor set away from trouble and only two away from disaster."

TECHNOLOGY ORGANIZATION

The senior vice president of technology at American Eagle is Michael Rempell, a former Andersen Consulting and Coopers & Lybrand consultant who has built the IT group to 60 people. Consisting of 10 to 15 people, each team serves specific functional areas: customer teams, product team, supply-chain team, and store operations. These IT teams are charged with helping functional leaders drive efficiencies, transparency, and productivity through and across functions. Like so many of the high-growth companies, American Eagle began in the design and supply-chain areas first, then moved to logistics, then moved to customers, then to store operations, and last to human resources.

STORE OPERATIONS

American Eagle store operations have several "be-better initiatives" under way under the direction of Joe Kerin, who began his career with the Silvermans. The first is the focus at the individual store level on:

- Customer experience
- Comps
- Conversion

This initiative is teaching store managers to staff, schedule, replenish inventory, and prioritize tasks that increase customer conversion and the size of the purchase by selling complementary or add-on products.

The second store initiative is for managers and directors to create moments of delight (MODs) for their customers. Managers are rewarded for and likewise can reward sales people daily for creating MOD customer experiences. Notice the proximity of the reward to the desired behavior.

American Eagle is instilling in its individual store managers the feeling that they "are owners of the shop," and as owners, they have the responsibility to treat all customers very, very well. The standard American Eagle is aiming for is to be the "Ritz Carlton of the retail industry."

Kerin is now focused on how best to communicate with and educate line employees about what the goals are, how to act to accomplish the goals, and how these actions translate into profits.

SUPPLY CHAIN

American Eagle has a Web-based supply-chain interface that links its in-house designers with its sourcing group, which gets bids from hundreds of manufacturing sources in 47 different countries. Bids are received quickly, and once a vendor is chosen, it is logged onto the American Eagle system so that the design group, supply-chain group, vendor oversight group, distribution, and store operations all have a real-time view of the time line, as well as the costs, including shipping, duties, and logistics costs. With the help of this system, the items are allocated to distribution centers and to stores by SKUs and colors. And by referencing the system, everyone knows what is coming in, how it is getting there (air or ocean), from where, when, and where it will arrive.

The second major project was a markdown-optimization program that focuses management on variances, which products are not moving, and where they are located.

THE PEOPLE CHALLENGE

American Eagle's people challenge is recruiting and retaining senior managers because it will lose its CEO and its vice chairman to retirement soon. It lost its CFO in July of 2005 to Ann Taylor, where she became COO. American Eagle has a strong middle-management bench but is challenged to prepare those people to lead into the next era.

At American Eagle, as at other organic growth stars, you see a progression from product focus to customer focus to, ultimately, people focus. And you see the progression from top-line focus to bottom-line focus to continuous be-better initiatives along the entire value chain.

It remains true to its roots, though, going so far as to announce plans to build its new corporate headquarters building in downtown Pittsburgh. Executives at American Eagle believe that being in Pittsburgh keeps them closer to their customers and helps them to stay focused and humble.

GROWTH QUESTIONS

1. What part of your value chain have you engineer-processed?
2. Which part of your value chain is technology-enabled to best of class?
3. How much productivity and efficiency margin can you generate from technology? 4 percent? 6 percent?
4. Do you receive real-time daily operational numbers?
5. How fast can you correct mistakes in execution?
6. How many be-better initiatives do you have ongoing now?
7. Are you an execution champion?

EPILOGUE

I DID NOT EXPECT THAT MY QUEST to find high organic growth companies would be difficult. In fact, when I began in 2002, I expected to find many, many companies that created substantial economic value primarily through organic growth. My model was designed to illuminate companies that created substantial economic value, primarily through organic growth—it was a demanding model. But I was surprised by the small number of companies that passed the various tests in each of my three studies. Earnings management and the creation of different types of earnings were more widespread than I expected—all caused by the fanatical focus on meeting quarterly earnings estimates.

And I as evaluated the high-performance organic companies, in an effort to understand how they were able to accomplish such results, I again expected to discover that these companies performed so well due to the commonly espoused theories of strategy, leadership, innovation, and globalization. Again, I discovered that this was not the case.

What I did find was that these organic growth companies are focused and disciplined companies obsessed with execution. Superior-execution companies are both great people companies and great technology companies. And as important, being top people companies did not lessen their performance in the slightest, as some might have expected.

My research produced four interesting results:

1. The six keys to organic growth.
2. The myths about what is necessary for high growth performance.
3. The organic growth progression followed by most of these companies.
4. The understanding that consistent organic growth requires a seamless systems approach—the consistent self-reinforcing linkage of strategy, culture, structure, accountability processes, execution processes, and people policies. Having a growth strategy alone is not enough. All parts have to be aligned and self-reinforcing.

These consistent high organic growth companies have iteratively and incrementally created an organic growth–generating system by focusing as much or even more on their internal processes as they do on the marketplace. And just as important, the humble leaders of these companies are focused on the details of operations.

These internal processes create a consistent, seamless, and self-reinforcing entrepreneurial environment in which line employees understand the business, understand their jobs, and are engaged and rewarded for performing consistently at their best. This results in employees becoming "owners" of their results and their careers. As a result, these employees are more loyal, productive, and committed.

Incremental improvement, employee engagement, engineering process, and technological enablement of the value chain are the blocking and tackling of execution excellence along the organic growth progression in these companies. This stuff is hard work. It is a daily focus on the details of execution.

These consistent high organic growth companies operate generally contrary to the popular management theories, which I call the *myths of organic growth*. What are generally accepted beliefs about the source of organic growth generally turned out to be false:

1. Contrary to popular belief, you do *not* need to have the best people to achieve high organic growth.
2. You do *not* necessarily need unique products or services. But you do need good-enough products, great customer service, and great execution.
3. You do *not* necessarily need to control a unique supply of raw materials or control a unique distribution channel.
4. You do *not* necessarily need sophisticated or diversified strategies. Instead, you need a strategy or business model that the average line employees can understand.
5. You do *not* necessarily need to be an innovation leader with big breakthrough discoveries. Constant iterative and incremental improvements are important for success.

6. You do *not* necessarily need to have the lowest labor costs.
7. You do *not* necessarily need to be global in scope.
8. You do *not* necessarily need to outsource or head off-shore.
9. You do *not* necessarily need an MBA to run your business.
10. You do *not* necessarily need a charismatic CEO.
11. You do *not* necessarily need to be located near talent, raw materials, or customers.

We found these oft-cited sources of competitive advantage to have little or no impact on building a company fueled by consistent organic growth.

The high organic growth companies keep the *big* things stable (strategy, the business model, leadership, and the internal rules of the game) while constantly improving the details of execution along the organic growth chain of progression. The successful companies teach us that it really is about execution—creating a system that produces high employee engagement, productivity, and loyalty, as well as a deep bench of humble operators as leaders who fight elitism, arrogance, hubris, complacency, and self-satisfaction.

The business world frequently is enamored of the machinations of strategy, financial engineering, conglomeration, deconglomeration, mergers, acquisitions, leveraged buyouts, charismatic leaders, and globalization, but I think we are on the leading edge of a return to the basics of business—execution and employee engagement.

However, I recognize that resistance to this return to

basics will be great—it is easier to create nonorganic earnings through accounting elections, valuations, or reserves or investment transactions, or financial engineering, or through mergers and acquisitions than through organic growth.

Great organic growth companies have learned how to use employees and technology to create highly efficient and productive organic growth machines. These companies stand for the proposition that employee engagement and the creation of substantial shareholder value are not mutually exclusive. Business is about execution, and execution only happens through and with people.

EMPLOYEE ENGAGEMENT

INPUT

- Hire for Fit
- Culture of Respect and Dignity
- Employees Understand Why and How Their Job is Important
- Frequent Feedback
- Consistent and Fair Accountability, Measurement, and Reward Policies
- Implied "Social Contract"–Stable Macro Corporate Environment
- Career Paths and Promote-from-Within Policies
- Entrepreneurial "Ownership"
- Humble Leaders as Role Models

OUTPUT
Better Retention
More Loyalty
Better Productivity
More Intensity
More Focus
More Discipline
More Trust

$

ENGAGING EMPLOYEES

These high organic growth companies also illuminated the importance of a systems approach to organic growth, engineering process, constant iterative and incremental improvement, technology enablement of the value chain, and promotion from within policies. Growth is more than a management strategy—it is a system, encompassing consistent strategy, culture, structure, execution processes, people policies and accountability, measurement and reward policies.

The high organic growth companies discussed here have learned how to harness the human spirit to pursue business excellence every day—day in and day out. Organic growth is entrepreneurial and is part of our American business history. It is time to return to the basics of business—growth the old-fashioned way.

APPENDIX

The Road to Organic Growth is supported by a number of observations about how high-growth companies achieve their level of success. By studying many of the 22 *organic growth index* (OGI) winners, we developed 69 chapter takeaways about leadership, growth strategies, and execution that you may find helpful.

1. Companies can create earnings many different ways.

2. Not all reported earnings represent the underlying strength and vitality of the core business.

3. The quality and character of reported earnings should be transparent to investors.

4. Organic growth is more representative of a company's viability and sustainability.

5. The organic growth index is an evolutionary model that discriminates between organic value creators and nonorganic value creators.

6. The organic growth index consists of six tests to illuminate high value creation primary through organic growth.

7. Twenty-two of more than 800 companies were organic growth winners in at least two of the three studies we conducted.

8. Less than 4 percent of the top economic value-added (EVA) creators for the time period 1996–2003 passed the six high organic growth performance tests.

9. There are 11 myths to being a consistent high organic growth company.

10. Employees executing every day at high levels of efficiency, productivity, and quality is mission-critical.

11. Business and management principles are simple—it is the consistent high-quality execution every day that is hard.

12. A sustainable competitive advantage is the seamless and consistent linkage and self-reinforcing interaction of the six keys.

13. Corporate location/geography does not seem to matter, which calls into question the theory of nodes of excellence.

14. At some point you would think that size would be an issue—but Wal-Mart has avoided this problem.

15. Great organic growth may be easier as companies move from small-cap through midcap to large-cap size.

16. Globalization is not a necessity; many of these companies are not global.

17. You do not necessarily need an MBA to lead a great organic growth company. Only 3 of the 22 CEOs have MBAs.

18. High-growth CEOs have worked, on average, more than 20 years at their companies, with 15 of the 22 having between 21 and 36 years of service.

19. All 22 companies have active stock buyback plans. They believe that they are good investments.

20. The high-growth companies are conservatively leveraged.

21. The organic growth manufacturers (PACCAR, Waters, Stryker, Tiffany, Harley-Davidson, and Mylan Laboratories) have production plants in the United States or Puerto Rico.

22. The 22 companies have business models and strategies that are simple, easy to explain, and easy to understand.

23. The companies have a disciplined focus on the business they know.

24. The companies evolve through iterative and incremental improvement.

25. Big innovations, new business models, and major change initiatives are not prevalent.

26. The line employee needs to understand the how and the why. He or she needs to understand how

his or her job creates value and why his or her job is important.

27. The U.S. Army K.I.S.S. principle applies: "Keep it simple, stupid."

28. These companies seem to go through a similar organic growth sequence.

29. First, they focus on top-line growth.

30. Then they focus on cost efficiencies and productivity.

31. A "small-company soul" is entrepreneurial.

32. Employees can be entrepreneurial when they have the authority, power, and responsibility to deal with customers and/or get results.

33. Taking ownership means being more engaged and committed.

34. "Small-company soul" means treating employees with respect and dignity and involving them in the process.

35. Small companies have a "family" feel to them.

36. In small companies, results count more than rules.

37. "Big-company body" means strong central controls from a financial, quality, legal, and results perspective.

38. Frequent measurements and feedback are necessary to control entrepreneurs.

39. Ownership also means fair financial rewards.

40. Mistakes will be made. The keys are to know about them quickly and fix them quickly.

41. Measurements are the key to accountability.

42. Frequent measurements are necessary to illuminate mistakes or problems.

43. Financial metrics are not enough.

44. Operational metrics that measure desired behaviors are critical.

45. The CFO is really the chief metrics officer (CMO).

46. Metrics need to be real-time and technology-based, and metrics need to be transparent throughout the organization.

47. Employees need to understand why certain measurements are important.

48. Measure the right things, and use metrics to have objective accountability, promotions, and financial rewards.

49. Building the people pipeline starts with hiring the right people.

50. High employee satisfaction is mission-critical.

51. Monetary pay by itself is not enough to truly engage employees.

52. Promotion from within is a key policy.

53. Stability and continuity of strategy and top management are common in these companies.

54. High-growth companies have different types of cultures, but all have consistent policies of treating employees like "owners" of their job, their customers, and the results of their performance.

55. All these companies show that they respect and care about their line employees.

56. Employee engagement policies and processes are a competitive advantage.

57. Many of these companies have an implied social contract with their employees: "You take care of the Company and the Company with take care of you."

58. The companies are primarily led by humble, passionate, focused operators.

59. Most of the leaders worked their way up the corporate ladder over a 20-year period.

60. Arrogance, hubris, and elitist perks of power are devalued by these CEOs.

61. The absence of MBAs at the top of most (19 of 22) of the companies is interesting.

62. The CEOs have not forgotten where they came from.

63. The CEOs value stewardship.

64. The CEOs are paranoid about failure on their watch.

65. The CEOs spent a significant amount of their time actually running the business.

66. Hire more engineers—engineering process is mission-critical.

67. To be great, you do not have to be perfect—but you need to be world class in technologically enabling your value chain.

68. World-class execution depends on (a) engaged employees, (b) the right accountability, measurement, and rewards systems, (c) a be-better entrepreneurial culture, and (d) technology enablement.

69. Technology enablement of the value chain drives information transparency in real time, real-time measurements, and operational efficiencies and productivity.

BIBLIOGRAPHY

ARTICLES

American Eagle Outfitters: "American Eagle Outfitters Soars to New Heights After a Reinvention," Jean E. Palmieri. December 9, 1998; copyright 1998 Fairchild Publications, Inc.

American Eagle Outfitters: "American Eagle Builds New Nests," Vicki M. Young. August 18, 1999; copyright 1999 Fairchild Publications, Inc.

American Eagle Outfitters: "American Eagle Outfitters. Inc.," March 12, 2003; copyright 2003 Market News Publishing, Inc.

American Eagle Outfitters: "American Eagle Outfitters Implement Web-based Global Sourcing from QRS," March 19, 2003, 2003 PR Newswire.

American Eagle Outfitters: "Updates: American Eagle Outfitters," March 1, 2005, Lebhar Friedman, Inc.

Automatic Data Processing: "Vendor Profile: Payroll Pioneer Making Inroads in CPA Arena," David McClure. September 20, 2004, Thomson Media, Inc.

Bed Bath & Beyond: "What's Beyond for Bed Bath & Beyond?" Nanette Byrnes. January 19, 2004, McGraw-Hill, Inc.

Bed Bath & Beyond: "Bed Bath & Beyond Continues to Grow Its Business One Item and One Market at a Time," Vanessa L. Facenda. March 1, 2004; copyright 2004 Gale Group, Inc.

Bed Bath and Beyond: "Bed Bath and Beyond: The Best at 'Playing house,' " Vanessa L. Facenda. July 1, 2004; copyright 2004 Gale Group, Inc.

Best Buy Co.: "Best Buy Outlines New Marketing Strategy," Scott Carlson. May 7, 2004, Knight Ridder Tribune Business News (KRTBN).

Best Buy Co.: "Company Profile Datamonitor," April 2005.

Best Buy Co.: "At Crossroads, Best Buy Charges Ahead with Customer Centricity," Laura Heller. January 10, 2005; copyright 2005 Gale Group, Inc.

Best Buy Co.: "Best Buy's Secret: Sales Staff," Carolyn Leitch. June 17, 2005, Bell Globemedia Publishing, Inc.

Best Buy Co.: "Brad Anderson: Best Buy Poised for Digital Future," Alan Wolf. October 25, 2004, Reed Business Information.

Best Buy Co.: Investor and Analyst Event: Final, Jennifer Driscoll, VP IR, Best Buy, October 19, 2005, Voxant FD Wire.

Best Buy Co., Inc., at Goldman Sachs 12th Annual Global Retailing Conference: Final, Matthew Fassler, Analyst, Goldman Sachs, September 9, 2005.

Best Buy Co.: "Who Will Buy It? The Nation's Largest Purveyor of Consumer Gadgets Hopes to Build Its Business by Tapping the Wallets of Jill, Barry, Buzz and Ray," Unmesh Kher. March 14, 2005, Time, Bell & Howell Information and Learning Company.

Best Buy Co.: "Best Buy Shapes Up the Big Box," Nisha Ramachandran. October 17, 2005, U.S. News and World Report.

Best Buy Co.: "Buying into a New Best Buy," Melessa Levy. Star Tribune, June 24, 2004.

Best Buy Co.: "Best Buy Re-aligns Its Resources to Support Three Growth Areas; President & COO Lenzmeier to Retire at the Start of Fiscal 1007," *Business Wire*, December 6, 2004.

Best Buy Co.; "In Retail, Profiling for Profit; Best Buy Stores Cater to Specific Customer Types," Ariana Eunjung Cha. *Washington Post*, August 17, 2005.

Brinker International: "Brinker Honoured with Mentor Award at Annual Elliot Leadership Confab," Dina Berta. May 23, 2005, Lebhar Friedman, Inc.

Brinker International: "Cultural Breakthrough," Justin Hibbard. September 21, 1998, CMP Media LLC.

Brinker International: "Executive Pay: My Big Fat Executive Pay Check," Claudia H. Deutsch. April 3, 2005, New York Times Company.

Family Dollar Stores: "Family Dollar Chairman Leaves Company Strong," Leigh Dyer. January 16, 2003, Knight Ridder Tribune Business News (KRTBN).

Family Dollar Stores: "Family Dollar Debuts Three Units in Utah," Debbie Howell. June 24, 2002, Gale Group, Inc.

Gentex Corp.: "Gentex Corp. Zealand, Michigan: Higher-Tech Mirrors Reflect Strong Growth," Marilyn Alva. September 24, 2002, *Investor's Business Daily*.

Harley-Davidson: "Harley-Davidson Growth Engine May Be Stalling," Ken Brown. February 12, 2002, Dow Jones & Company, Inc.

Harley-Davidson: "Riding Toward New Markets: Beyond the Boomers, Andra Maria Cecil. July 17, 2005, Bell & Howell Information and Learning Company.

Harley-Davidson: "Ready to Roll: Harley-Davidson's Three-Year Effort to Build Close Ties to Suppliers Is Paying Off," Laurie Sullivan. March 8, 2004, CMP Media LLC.

Harley-Davidson: "Harley Davidson, Inc., Datamonitor," September 2005.

Harley-Davidson: "How Harley-Davidson & Its Suppliers Collaborate to Reduce Inventory," April 1, 2003, Institute of Management & Administration.

Harley-Davidson: "How Harley-Davidson Teamed with 16 Major Suppliers to Cut Costs," January 1, 2003, Institute of Management & Administration.

Maggiano Little Italy: "Yorgo Koutsogiorgas Keeps Maggiano's Turnover Down with Upbeat Culture," Dina Berta. August 11, 2003, Gale Group, Inc.

Mylan Laboratories: Mylan Laboratories, Inc., copyright proxy statement persuant section 14(a).

Omnicom: "An Empire of Happy Fiefdoms," Diane Brady. April 3, 2000, McGraw-Hill, Inc.

Omnicom: "Omnicom CEO Breaks Advertising Mold," Vanessa O. Connell. November 15, 2000, Dow Jones & Company, Inc.

Omnicom: "Omnicom Lets Agencies Do the Talking: Corporate Reorganization," Gary Silverman. March 15, 2005, Financial Times Group.

Omnicom: "Omnicom in Market for Damage Limitation," Richard Tomkins. June 16, 2002, Financial Times Group.

Omnicom: "What Advertising Downturn? Omnicom's John Wren Thrives While Rivals Writhe," Melanie Wells. January 7, 2002, Forbes, Inc.

Omnicom: "Omnicom Group, Inc., Datamonitor," May 2005.

Outback Steakhouse: "A Marketing Legend Steps Down," Robert Trigaux., March 9, 2005, *St. Petersburg Times.*

Ross Stores: "Dressing More for Less: Ross Store, July 1, 2002, Gale Group, Inc., Racher Press, Inc.

Ross Stores: "Ross Stores Promotes Key Merchandising and Operating Executives," February 8, 2005, PR Newswire Association LLC.

Stryker Corp.: "Stryker to Buy Pfizer Unit for $1.9 Billion," Steven Lipin. August 14, 1998, Dow Jones & Company, Inc.

Stryker Corp.: "Conservative Stryker Joins the Merger Game in a Big Way," James P. Miller. August 21, 1998, Dow Jones & Company, Inc.

Stryker Corp.: "CEO Expects to Leave Stryker in Good Hands," Jane Parikh. March 16, 2003.

Tiffany & Co.: "Best of Leaders & Success Charles Tiffany," Katie Sweeney. October 6, 2004, *Investor's Business Daily*.

Total System Services: "TSYS Makes Payment Inroads Against First Data," Lavonne Kuykendall. November 3, 2004, Thomson Media, Inc.

Total System Services: "Retail Banking: Big Steals from a Safe Giant-TSYS," May 1, 2003, *The Banker*.

Walgreen Co.: "Developing Careers, People Through Human Resources," Bruce Buckley. October 16, 2000, Gale Group, Inc.

Walgreen Co.: "Cultivating a Deep Talent Pool Dedicated to Long Term Goals," James Frederick. March 22, 2004, Gale Group, Inc.

Walgreen Co.: "Leading the Way with Record Profits," James Frederick. April 24, 2000, Information Access Company.

Walgreen Co.: "Pursuing Topflight Services, Achieving Superior Operations," James Frederick. March 22, 2004, Gale Group, Inc.

Walgreen Co.: "Perfecting the Standard," Laura Heller. April 29, 2002, Gale Group, Inc.

Walgreen Co.: "Promoting from Within Turns Experience into Advantage," Michelle L. Kirsche. March 22, 2004, Gale Group, Inc.

Walgreen Co.: "How Walgreen Rallied to the Aid of Terminally Ill Purchasing Agent," Ted Pincus. March 2, 2004, Bell & Howell Information and Learning Company.

Walgreen Co.: "Cork Walgreen Shapes Industry's Top Chain," December 15, 1997, Racher Press, Inc.

Walgreen Co.: "Positive Productive People Are Key to Walgreens Success," October 16, 2000, Gale Group, Inc.

Walgreen Co.: "Succession Plan Relies on Deep Talent Pool," March 23, 2003, Gale Group, Inc.

Walgreen Co.: "Quality Management at Every Level," December 15, 2003, Gale Group, Inc.

Walgreen Co.: "Realignment Paves Way for Walgreens' Growth," February 14, 2000, Gale Group, Inc.

Walgreen Co.: "Jorndt Era Marked by Growth," December 16, 2002, Gale Group, Inc.

Walgreen Co.: "Making Drug Stores the Focus," December 15, 1997, Racher Press, Inc.

Walgreen Co.: "Rx for Growth: Walgreens Shares Are Down, But Its Prospects Are Bright: A Winning Prescription?" Harish S. Bryne. January 4, 2002, Dow Jones & Company, Inc.

Walgreen Co.: "Walgreen Ties up 30 Sites: Drug Wars Escalate," *Matt Roush Crain's Detroit Business,* September 8, 1997, Crain Communications, Inc.

Walgreen Co.: "A Century of Growth Comes Full Circle," Rob Eder. October 16, 2000, Gale Group, Inc.

Walgreen Co.: "Weathering a Tough Economy, Walgreen Maintains Its Streak," Frederick James. October 20, 2003, Gale Group, Inc.

Walgreen Co.: "Powerhouse Profits Feed Growth Juggernaut," Frederick James. April 19, 2004, Gale Group, Inc.

Walgreen Co.: "Selling the Quick Trip to the 'Corner Pharmacy,' " Molly Prior. March 22, 2004, Gale Group, Inc.

Walgreen Co.: "Walgreens Sees Everything in Terms of Its Customers," December 16, 2002, Gale Group, Inc.

Walgreen Co.: "Walgreens Shuns Feeding Frenzy, Thrives on Growth Company Profile," April 27, 1998, Gale Group, Inc.

Wal-Mart: "Wal-Mart Growth Seen as Burdening California, Arkansas," Alex Daniels. August 22, 2004, Arkansas Democrat-Gazette, Inc.

Wal-Mart: "An Appreciation for People," Steve Bates. October 1, 2003, Bell & Howell Information and Learning Company.

Wal-Mart: "FT Interview, Lee Scott, CEO of Wal-Mart," Niel Buckley. January 7, 2003, Financial Times Group.

Wal-Mart: "Wal-Mart Tries on Fashion Apparel: Fashion Can Be Risky," Howard L. Davidowitz. February 1, 2004, Gale Group, Inc.

Wal-Mart: "The Observer Profile: Lee Scott, Market Leader," Paul Harris. September 12, 2004, *The Observer.*

Wal-Mart: "Driving Wal-Mart's Growth Engine: A Dramatic Shift," Art Turock. February 1, 2004, Gale Group, Inc.

Wal-Mart: "Wal-Mart Proofing the Store: Picking the Right Target Customers," Art Turock. May 1, 2003, Gale Group, Inc.

Wal-Mart: "Wal-Mart Inches Way into Japan," Yumiko Ono. March 15, 2002, Dow Jones & Company, Inc.

Wal-Mart: "Interview: Lee Scott Discusses Wal-Mart and Its Future," March 31, 2004, *The Tavis Smiley Show.*

Wal-Mart: "Big Companies Become Big Targets Unless They Guard Images Carefully," Carol Hymowitz. December 12, 2005, *Wall Street Journal.*

Waters Corp.: "Waters Corp. Does Global ERP in 99 Days," Deborah Gage. October 1, 2003, Ziff Davis Media, Inc.

Waters Corp.: "Patents Suits Entangle Millford, Mass," Jeffrey Krasner. May 22, 2002, Knight Ridder Tribune Business News (KRTBN).

Waters Corp.: "Healthy Signs for an Instrument Maker: S&P," Jeffrey Loo. July 20, 2004, McGraw-Hill, Inc.

Waters Corp.: "Waters' Rise and How It Plans to Stay on Top," February 29, 2002, Information Access Company.

Waters Corp.: "Centralized Data Management for Greater Control and Compliance," Mark Harnois. August 1, 2005, Reed Business Information.

Collins, Jim. "Level 5 Leadership: The Triumph of Humility and Fierce Resolve," *HBR*, January 2001, pp. 66–76.

Collis, David and Cynthia Montgomery. "Creating Corporate Advantage," *HBR*, May–June 1998, pp. 70–83.

Couter, Diane L. "Sense and Reliability—A Conversation with Celebrated Psychologist Karl E. Werck," *HBR*, April 2003, pp. 84–90.

Pearson, Andrall E. "Touch-Minded Ways to Get Innovative," *HBR*, August 2002, pp. 117–124.

Rogers, Paul, Tom Holland, and Dan Haas. "Value Acceleration: Lessons from Private Equity Masters," *HBR*, June 2002, pp. 94–101.

Slywotsky, Adrian andRichard Wise. "The Growth Crisis and How to Escape It," *HBR*, July 2002, pp. 72–83.

BOOKS

Badaracco, Joseph L. Jr. *Leading Quietly*. HBS Press, 2002. ISBN 1-57851-487-8.

Bennis, Warren G. and Robert J Thomas. *Geeks and Geezers*. HBS Press, 2002. ISBN 1-57851-582-3.

Bethune, Gordon. *From Worst to First.* Wiley, 1998. ISBN 0-417-24835-5.

Bossidy, Larry and Ram Charan. *Execution: The Discipline of Getting Things Done.* Crown Business, 2002. ISBN 0-609-61057-0.

Bruner, Robert F. *Deals from Hell: M&A Lessons That Rise Above the Ashes.* Wiley, 2005. ISBN 13 978-0471-39595-9.

Buckingham, Marcus, and Curt Coffman. *First, Break All the Rules.* Simon and Schuster, 1999. ISBN 0-684-85285-1.

Christensen, Clayton M. *The Innovator's Dilemma.* HBS Press, 1997. ISBN 0-87584585-1.

Collins, Jim. *Good to Great.* Harper Business, 2001. ISBN 0-06-662099-6.

Copeland, Tom, Tim Koller, and Jack Murrin. *Valuation: Measuring and Managing the Value of Companies,* 2d ed. Wiley, 1994. ISBN 0-471-36190-9.

D'Aveni, Richard. *Hypercompetition.* Free Press, 1994. ISBN 0029069386.

Dell, Michael, and Catherine Fredman. *Direct from Dell.* Harper Business, 1999. ISBN 0-88730-914-3.

Eichenwalk, Kurt. *Conspiracy of Fools: A True Story.* Broadway Books, 2005. ISBN 0-7679-1178-4.

Finkelstein, Sydney. *Why Smart Executives Fail.* Postfolio Books, 2003. ISBN 1-59184-010-4.

Fridson, Martin, Fernando Alvarez, and Martin S. Fridson. *Financial Statement Analysis: A Practitioner's Guide,* 3d ed. Wiley, 2002. ISBN 0-471-40915-4.

Goleman, Daniel, Richard Boyatzis, and Annie McKee. *Primal Leadership: Learning to Lead with Emotional Intelligence.* HBS Press, 2002. ISBN 1-57851-486-X.

Greenleaf, Robert K. I. *Servant Leadership: Essays.* Paulist Press, 2002. ISBN 0-8091-0554-3.

Hargadon, Andrew. *How Breakthroughs Happen.* HBS Press, 2003. ISBN 1-57851-904-7.

Heskett, James L., Earl W. Sasser, Jr., and Leonard A. Schlesinger. *The Value Profit Chain.* Free Press, 2003. ISBN 0-7432-2569-4.

Hess, Edward D., and Kim S. Cameron, eds. *Leading with Values: Positivity, Virtue and High Performance.* Cambridge University Press, 2006. ISBN 0-521-68603-2.

Hess, Edward D., and Robert K. Kazanjian, eds. *The Search for Organic Growth.* Cambridge University Press, 2006. ISBN 0-521-85260-9.

Joyce, William, Nitin Nohria, and Bruce Roberson. *What Really Works: The 4+2 Formula for Sustained Business Success.* Harper Business, 2003. ISBN 0-06-051278-4.

Kaplan, Robert S., and David P. Norton. *The Balanced Scorecard: Translating Strategy into Action.* HBS Press, 1996. ISBN 0-87584-651-3.

Knight, Charles F., and Davis Dyer. *Performance without Compromise.* HBS Press, 2005. ISBN 1-59139-777-47432-0560-X.

Kotler, Philip. *Kotler on Marketing.* Free Press, 1999. ISBN 0-68-85033-8.

Lipton, Mark. *Guiding Growth.* HBS Press, 2003. ISBN 1-57851-706-0.

McGrath, Rita, and Ian C. MacMillan. *The Entrepreneurial Mindset.* HBS Press, 2000. ISBN 0-87584-834-6.

McLean, Bethany, and Peter Elkind. *The Smartest Guys in the Room: The Amazing Rise and Scandalous Fall of Enron.* Penguin, 2003. ISBN 1-59184-008-2.

Magretta, Joan. *What Management Is.* Free Press, 2002. ISBN 0-7432-0318-6.

Marcus, Bernie, and Arthur Blank, with Bob Andelman. *The Home Depot.* Time Business, 1999. ISBN 0-8129-3058-4.

Mintzberg, Henry, Bruce Ahistrand, and Joseph Lampel. *Strategy Safari: A Guided Tour Through the Wilds of Strategic Management.* Prentice-Hall, 1998. ISBN 0-13695677-7.

O'Reilly, Charles A., and Jeffrey Pfeffer. *Hidden Value.* HBS Press, 2000. ISBN 0-87584-898-2

Porter, Michael E. *Competitive Strategy.* Free Press, 1980. ISBN 0-02-025360-8.

Schilit, Howard. *Financial Shenanigans: How to Detect Accounting Gimmicks and Fraud in Financial Reports,* 2d ed. McGraw-Hill, 2002. ISBN 0-07-138626-2.

Schultz, Howard, and Dori Jones Yang. *Pour Your Heart into It.* Hyperion, 1997. ISBN 0-7868-6397-8.

Sheth, Jagdish, and Rajendra Sisofia. *The Rule of Three: Surviving and Thriving in Competitive Markets.* Free Press, 2002. ISBN 0-

Slywotsky, Adrian, and Rickland Wise. *How to Grow When Markets Don't.* Warner, 2003, ISBN 0-446-69270-0

Stewart, James B. *Disney War.* Simon & Schuster, 2005. ISBN 0-684-80993-1.

Sullivan, Gordon R., and Michael V. Harper. *Hope Is Not a Method.* Broadway Books, 1996. ISBN 0-7679-0060-4.

Teerlink, Rich, and Lee Ozley. *More Than a Motorcycle.* HBS Press, 2000. ISBN 0-87584-950-4.

Treacy, Michael. *Double-Digit Growth.* Portfolio, 2003. ISBN 1-59184-005-8.

Truett, S. Cathy. *Eat More Chiken; Inspire More People.* Chick-fil-A, Inc., 2002. ISBN 1-929619-08-1.

Walton, Sam, and John Huey. *Sam Walton: Made in America.* Bantam Books, 1993; Doubleday Edition, 1992. ISBN 0-553-56283-5

AUTHOR'S COMMENTARIES: FOUND AT WWW.EDHLTD.COM

"The Silver Bullet of Leadership," *The Catalyst*, November 2004.

"Corporate Social Responsibility: The Value of Business Stewardship," *The Catalyst*, October 2004.

"Entrepreneurs: Reality vs. Myth," *The Catalyst*, July 2004.

"Managing VUCA," *The Catalyst*, June 2004.

"Are Your Employees a Means to Your End?" *The Catalyst*, May 2004.

"When Should Your Business Stop Growing," *The Catalyst*, March 2004.

"Blocking and Tackling," *The Catalyst*, December 2003.

"What Do Good Leaders Actually Do?" Part II, *The Catalyst*, November 2003.

"What Is the Meaning of Business?" *The Catalyst*, October 2003.

"What Do Good Leaders Actually Do?" Part I, *The Catalyst*, September 2003.

"Do You Have a Broken Arrow Plan?" *The Catalyst*, August 2003.

"Rapid Growth: Be Careful What You Ask For," *The Catalyst*, July 2003.

"Entrepreneurial Leadership: Why Should Anyone Follow You?" *The Catalyst*, June 2003.

"Why Successful Companies Often Fail," *The Catalyst*, February 2003.

"Managing Execution," *The Catalyst*, January 2003.

INDEX

ABOUT THE AUTHOR

Edward D. Hess, B.S., J.D., L.L.M., is an adjunct professor of organization and management, and the founder and executive director of both The Center for Entrepreneurship and Corporate Growth, and the Values-Based Leadership Institute at the Goizueta Business School at Emory University. Hess's research on organic growth has been featured in the *Financial Times, Fortune Magazine,* and on Fortune.com. Professor Hess was a senior executive at Warburg, Paribas Becker, Boettcher & Company, Jones Lang Wooten, and Andersen Finance. He is a graduate of the University of Virginia (J.D.) and New York University (L.L.M.), and the author of Hess & Cameron, eds., *Leading with Values: Positivity, Virtue & High Performance* (Cambridge U Press, 2006), along with 40 articles, and three other books. For more information, visit him on the Web at www.edhltd.com.